中国外籍教师英语教学教程
TEACHING ENGLISH AS A FOREIGN LANGUAGE IN CHINA TODAY

Benjamin Duncan, Ph. D. Center for Teaching & Learning in China
Liu Shusen 刘树森, Ph. D. Peking University
De-an Wu Swihart 吴德安, Ph. D. Center for Teaching & Learning in China
William H. O'Donnell, Ph. D. Center for Teaching & Learning in China

图书在版编目(CIP)数据

中国外籍教师英语教学教程/(美)邓肯(Duncan, B.),刘树森,(美)吴德安,(美)欧比尔(O'Donnell. W. H.)编著. —北京:北京大学出版社,2013.8
ISBN 978-7-301-21313-1

Ⅰ.中… Ⅱ①邓… ②刘… ③吴… ④欧… Ⅲ.英语—教学法—教材 Ⅳ. H319.3

中国版本图书馆 CIP 数据核字(2012)第 230477 号

Do not reproduce in any form without the advance written permission of Center for Teaching & Learning in China LLC(china.program@gmail.com) and each of the authors
Preface & Chapters 1–17 ⓒ 2012 Benjamin Duncan
Chapter 18 ⓒ 2012 Liu Shusen
Chapter 19 ⓒ 2012 De-an Wu Swihart & William H. O'Donnell

书　　　　名:	中国外籍教师英语教学教程
著作责任者:	[美]Benjamin Duncan,刘树森,[美]De-an Wu Swihart,[美]William H. O'Donnell 编著
责 任 编 辑:	黄瑞明
标 准 书 号:	ISBN 978-7-301-21313-1/H·3148
出 版 发 行:	北京大学出版社
地　　　　址:	北京市海淀区成府路 205 号　100871
网　　　　址:	http://www.pup.cn
电　　　　话:	邮购部 62752015　发行部 62750672　编辑部 62754382　出版部 62754962
电 子 信 箱:	zbing@pup.pku.edu.cn
印 刷 者:	涿州市星河印刷有限公司
经 销 者:	新华书店
	787 毫米×1092 毫米　16 开本　11.75 印张　306 千字
	2013 年 8 月第 1 版　2013 年 8 月第 1 次印刷
定　　　　价:	35.00 元

未经许可,不得以任何方式复制或抄袭本书之部分或全部内容。
版权所有,侵权必究
举报电话: 010-62752024　电子信箱: fd@pup.pku.edu.cn

TABLE OF CONTENTS

Preface 1

Chapter 1   Expectations 1
Chapter 2   What Is Language Teaching? 4
Chapter 3   Lesson Planning 18
Chapter 4   Adapting and Revising Lesson Plans 25
Chapter 5   Language Acquisition 37
Chapter 6   Multiple Intelligences 45
Chapter 7   Methodology 51
Chapter 8   Nine Principles of TEFL 59
Chapter 9   Classroom Management 68
Chapter 10   Teaching Primary School 76
Chapter 11   Reading and Vocabulary 85
Chapter 12   Speaking and Listening 98
Chapter 13   Pronunciation 114
Chapter 14   Grammar-Based Lessons 136
Chapter 15   Writing 143
Chapter 16   Error Correction 153
Chapter 17   Cultural Differences 158
Chapter 18   English in China's Educational System 164
Chapter 19   Living and Teaching in China: Tips for Teachers 169

References 181

Preface

Teaching English as a Foreign Language in China Today has been developed through 16 years of experience in training more than 1,000 foreign teachers of English by the Center for Teaching & Learning in China (CTLC), in cooperation with the Peking University English Department and School of Foreign Languages. Benjamin Duncan, Ph.D. wrote this book at the invitation of CTLC and as a CTLC trainer. He first taught English in China in 1999 with the CTLC program in Shenzhen. This book builds upon CTLC's 2007 textbook Teaching English in China, written by CTLC trainers, Robert Wyss, M.A. and Emily A. Thrush, Ph.D., and CTLC Co-Directors De-an Wu Swihart, Ph.D. and William O'Donnell, Ph.D., and with an appendix provided by the Department of Culture & Education of the State Administration of Foreign Expert Affairs, which officially endorsed the book and uses it in their training.

Teaching English as a Foreign Language in China Today is very useful for English teachers to learn how to teach English in China. It includes chapters written by highly experienced professors from the USA and from Chinese faculty of the Peking University English Department. The emphasis on understanding Chinese culture addresses the needs of foreign teachers living in China.

De-an Wu Swihart, Ph.D., Co-Director, CTLC
William O'Donnell, Ph.D., Co-Director, CTLC
Liu Shusen, Ph.D., Associate Dean, School of Foreign Language, Peking University

Greetings from Benjamin Duncan

Laoshimen hao! Hello, teachers! If you've never heard this greeting before, get used to it! Welcome to the wonderful world of TEFL teaching. Many people travel to China for vacation, but you have chosen to live and work in China. Not only live and work, but live and work in one of the most prestigious positions in Chinese culture: teaching. Teachers provide a manifest benefit to the surrounding community for they help its children to increase their knowledge, understanding, and wisdom of the events and community into which they develop. Yes, that's right—you are now a part of the Chinese community. Your work, knowledge and skills will provide economic, social, and political benefit to the students that you teach, your co-workers, and their families. Rather than remaining safely within your culture, you have chosen to look outside and into other cultures for answers to your future. You are seeking to expand your border and gain a new community.

In 1999, I taught in the first full year of the CTLC Shenzhen English Teaching Program. In 2001, I had the chance to revisit my school, Pingang Middle School in Longgang, and my former co-workers. I'll never forget what the vice-principal told me. After one year of TEFL teaching in China, you were an American English teacher, but when you return, you are now Chinese. Although I would never call myself Chinese, I do after all these years maintain a sense of community and empathy toward those I befriended and worked with over the course of my year teaching in Shenzhen.

CTLC aims to provide an additional community to you while living and working in China. We are the largest TEFL program in China and serve you with both social and professional support. Yes, you are now a professional! As such, we hope that you will take your professional responsibilities and your expected contributions to your new community quite seriously. This next year will be what you make of it, but I strongly hope that you will make it more than just a trip through China. I hope you will feel pride in being a teacher, a *laoshi*, and a contributive part of your new community.

This textbook is designed to help guide your professional development in the world of TEFL teaching. We hope that you will keep this book with you at all times and refer to it quite often as you begin your new career. The topics covered herein include expectations, language acquisition theory, lesson planning, strategies for teaching reading, writing, speaking, and listening, classroom management, teaching primary school, adapting lessons for different levels, cultural differences, and more. Throughout you will find anecdotes from current and former instructors in the program that should enlighten and prepare you for what's to come. But that's what's to come. For now, just soak in your new environment and the future that's about to unfold before your eyes. Welcome to China! *Laoshimen hao*!

Sincerely,
Benjamin R. Duncan, Ph.D.
CTLC Teacher Trainer

Expectations

Chapter 1

The goals for this chapter are:
> To introduce yourself to the other new teachers in the program.
> To set achievable goals for your time in China.
> To set achievable goals for your new career as a TEFL teacher.

Reflection:

I entered the TEFL in China program in 1999, the first full year of the program. I had never taught before, had never studied Chinese, had never been outside of the U. S., and had no idea what to expect. I remember waking up the first day, around 5am due to jet lag, and going for a walk. There were no signs posted in English and no one I could talk to to ask for help. Store owners and students hustled about. They were dressed in clothes very different from my printed T-shirt and khaki shorts. They rode rickety bicycles, walked quickly, and spoke in Chinese, a singsong language that sounded completely alien to

my ears. I had made my way to the Peking University campus, and was looking over a large lake covered in a thick mist. Suddenly, rising out of the mist, I saw about 300 men and women practicing tai chi in absolute silence. Their movements, in perfect unison, seemed to carve the air and direct some invisible energy from the surrounding lake. Another member from our **TEFL in China** program, who I had briefly met at the airport, came jogging toward me. We looked at each other, looked at the scene below us and smiled. This was another world. This was a dreamlike experience unlike anything we had ever seen or imagined before. And this was only the start of a full year of cultural learning. This was China.

Introductions

Please fill in the chart below with your own information and information from two people seated near you.

Names			
Tell me about yourself			
Why did you come to China?			
Where else have you travelled?			
Do you speak Chinese/other languages?			
What about teaching in China scares you the most?			
What are your expectations for living and working in China?			
What is one thing that you would like to see or do during your year in China?			

Your Personal Expectations

Some of the joys of living in a foreign country are that it changes your perceptions, challenges your prejudices, and ultimately forces you to grow as a human being. Whatever you think of

Chapter 1 Expectations

China and TEFL teaching today is likely to be very different by next year. Take a few moments to record your own private and personal expectations for the upcoming year. You won't be asked to share your responses, but I'd like you to keep this book in a safe place. At the end of your year in China, revisit your answers and see whether or not your expectations were realized.

1. What do you expect living in China to be like? List at least three expectations you have in order of importance.

2. What do you expect teaching English in Chinese classrooms is like? List at least three expectations you have in order of importance.

3. What skills or personal qualities do you believe characterize successful foreign language instructors?

4. What aspects of classroom teaching do you expect to find the most challenging? What about your teaching experience will be the most rewarding?

5. What questions do you have about teaching English in China? Can you provide preliminary answers to those questions?

6. How will you change in the next year? What do you expect to learn?

Deputy director of Culture and Education Department of China Foreign Expert Bureau with CTLC faculties

What Is Language Teaching?

Chapter 2

The goals for this chapter are to learn:
- How does the mind actually acquire language? How does this affect the way we teach a second language?
- What does it mean to be fluent in a second language compared to a first language?
- Given our understanding of language acquisition and some sample activities, how can we expand the knowledge from this workshop to create our own materials and lessons?

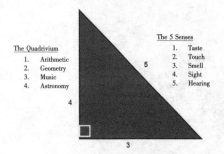

Reflection:

In ancient times, the world was a mysterious place. The sun would disappear at times; darkness would envelop the land only to dissolve several hours later. Brilliant points of illumination would prick the sky, shifting with the seasons and sometimes falling in a spray of light. Floods, droughts, abundant harvests, fires, ice storms, mist... the world was ever-changing and its laws unintelligible to mortal beings. Some plants tasted bad

Chapter 2 What Is Language Teaching?

but warded off disease; others smelled wonderful but produced sickness. Sounds reverberated and became harmonious under some settings, but were muffled and discordant under others. Touching certain objects produced observable, biological reactions in both the actor and the acted upon, while touching other objects resulted in no change at all. Moreover, senses differed among individuals. What smelled, looked, sounded good to one did not always smell, look, and sound good to another. Individuals tried to discern their surroundings through the only resources available to them: the five senses.

But humans also had another resource which separated them from all other creatures on Earth: language. Innately, humans could move their lips, tongue, teeth, and vocal cords to produce sounds. And what's more amazing is that the recipients of these sounds could process them, separate them from other sounds, find meaning in them, and pass them along to other human beings. Individuals could communicate their sensory perceptions to others. Knowledge was spread; lives were saved; communities arose; the world became more predictable-all as a result of language.

Legend says that the first schools developed spontaneously throughout the ancient world (Babylon, Sumer, India, Egypt, Greece, and South America). Initiates into these so-called mystery schools were taught the hidden laws of the universe and language. The most famous scholar of these various mystery schools, Pythagoras, is said to have been inducted into certain rights that led him to the creation of modern geometry. Before Pythagoras, few knew how to construct a right angle. Protractors and GPS did not exist, and the land and sea were far from flat and straight, so how was one to know what was perfectly "right" and what was slightly off center? Without right angles, navigation and architecture were puzzling if not impossible tasks. However, knowledge of the elementary coefficients 3, 4, and 5 allowed initiates like Pythagoras to tangibly improve their technological tools, their surroundings, as a result, their understanding of life and nature. For example, Grecian ships were universally constructed 3 units from helm to mast, 4 units from the bottom of the mast to the top, and 5 units from the top of the mast back to the helm. Thus, a right angle was created allowing the ship's navigator to accurately calculate distance and time between two fixed points. Travel and trade flourished and the societies of ancient Greece along with them. However, the 3, 4, 5 principle had a deeper meaning to those initiated into the mystery schools.

The first plank of the classical liberal education focused solely on language and was known as the trivium (3), consisting of grammar, logic, and rhetoric. Grammar involves basic **knowledge** of a language: the who, what, when, and where. (Modern grammarians complicate grammar with terms like subject, agent, predicate, theme, modifiers, adjunct, etc. but basically grammar is just breaking down language into meaningful expression of who, what, when, and where). Using our five senses, we look at/smell/listen to/touch/taste the world and attempt to make meaning of it. We see somebody approaching us. "*Who* is that?" we ask. An enemy, a lover, an ex-lover, a drunken, crazed, and gun-bearing ex-lover, two drunken, crazed, and gun-bearing ex-lovers? The who (or subject) is meaningful—it affects our perception of the situation. "*What* are they doing?" we then ask. *They are attacking us* is very different from *they are being attacked by us;*

they are pretending to love us is very different from *they love us*. The what (or verb/theme) is also meaningful. "*When* is this action taking place?" we might ask. *He will die* is very different from *he died*. The when (or tense/aspect) is meaningful. "*Where* is this happening?" our senses seek to answer. *I am walking into the sea* is very different from *I am walking on the sea*. *I am sleeping above Dave* is very different from *I am sleeping with Dave*. All languages contain grammar. The order of words, the structure of langue is important as it contains clues to the meaning. *I hit the desk* differs significantly from *The desk hits me*. Without grammar it would be nearly impossible for humans to accurately communicate **knowledge** of their perceptions to others and to make their communications meaningful. According to classical liberal education, the first part of learning a language is to gain knowledge of (i.e., break down) the *who, what, when,* and *where* of the language being spoken or written.

But how do we know if what is being spoke or written is true? If it is merely personal opinion or if it is a universal fact? Or if the communication is meant as a joke, or is an attempt to persuade, or is a propagandistic lie? To **understand** what is being spoken or written means to go beyond mere grammar to question, the purpose, intended effect, and reason behind that communication. In nature no contradictions exist; however, human perception and language is full of contradictions. Thus, pupils require a system to ferret out fact from fiction. Such a system is known as logic.

Finally, once we possess **knowledge** and **understanding** of how a particular language works, we can communicate meaningfully our own perceptions and thoughts. Rhetoric is the art of communicating effectively, the **wisdom** to pass along one's knowledge and understanding of the world to others and have it be accepted as meaningful and of value. Primary education under the classical system focused solely on language learning; however, once the **knowledge**, **understanding**, and **wisdom** of linguistic communication were acquired, the student could discern reality for him or herself. Thus, individuals trained in the trivium could acquire all other subjects faster, could retain them longer, and required less direct instruction or rote memorization than students not trained in grammar, logic, and rhetoric. In ancient Greece there were only four secondary subjects, aka the quadrivium: arithmetic (the study of logic through numbers), geometry (the study of numbers in space), music (the study of numbers in time), and astronomy (the study of numbers in both time and space). Students trained in the trivium and quadrivium gained a clearer perception of their world and were able to communicate their individual senses to others. They were able to question and counter the falsities, illogical conclusions, and duplicitous expressions of others. They became independent, free, liberal thinkers rather than slaves to another's words and ideas. In other words, they learned the "right" way of thinking and communicating.

It's like two students learning to play Beethoven's *Fifth Symphony* on the piano. The first music teacher drills the new student into memorizing and repeating the *Fifth Symphony* over and over again. The second music teacher instructs her student how to read music, proper finger position, scales, etc. and then, and only then with this basic knowledge, begins work on Beethoven's *Fifth*. Obviously, the first student will learn faster and after maybe several months the end product will appear more impressive to a casual listener; however, when it comes to learn another piece of music, say Beethoven's *Fourth*, the first student will also be more dependent on the teacher than the second. The new piece will have to be memorized and repeated same as the first and similarly every new piece of music that follows. Meanwhile, the second student learns the second piece faster than the first, the following piece faster than the second, and so on. Eventually, the second student internalizes the process for playing *any* piece of music, relies less and less on the teacher, and begins to create his or her own music. This is what is meant by educators when we say **learning a language is a process, not a product**. Unfortunately, a large number of language teachers, myself included, initially fail to comprehend this very important and simple concept. You can quickly become one of the best TESOL teachers by learning and applying the "right" theories for language learning.

1st Language Acquisition Is Innate

Did your parents ever sit you down and explain to you the rules of English grammar? Did they explicate the conjugation of verbs or how to differentiate between the various prepositions (e.g. "from" vs. "of")? Did they diagram the sentences that they spoke, detail the various tenses and aspects, or train you to record and analyze the speech of linguistic experts? Likely, the answer is no. And yet, all human beings achieve fluency and accuracy in their native language at a relatively young age.

Now, let's imagine (easier for some than others) that at birth your parents had sold you on the black market to another family in China, Spain, or France. What language do you think you'd be speaking today? Would you speak that language fluently? Obviously, you'd be fluent speaker of Chinese, Spanish, or French. How and why does this happen?

When it comes to language acquisition, the human mind is faster, smarter, and more nuanced than any teaching technique, linguistic theory, or technological device could ever hope to become. This is a result of thousands if not hundreds of thousands of years of evolution and natural selection. The human species is not unique in that our ancestry has replicated, mutated, and adapted to its environment. What is unique about our species is that our primary evolutionary trait is language. Elephants have a nose that can breathe, grasp objects, drink, fight, and nurture children. Squirrels have a mind that can remember the exact location of up to 100 different objects. Humans have language.

Steven Pinker's *How the Mind Works, The Blank Slate,* and *The Language Instinct* are great, easy-to-read books for new language teachers and have informed much of my own understanding of 2nd language acquisition. Take a simple quote you have heard many times before: "That's one small step for man, one giant leap for mankind." What's involved in our understanding of this quote? First, we need to **understand** the grammar of the sentence. What's the subject? *That*. What does *that* mean? To what does *that* refer (the beneficiary)? What's the verb (theme)? *Is* ('s) = to be, present tense. What does that comma signify? What follows the comma? What does that associative noun clause (aka oblique adjunct) refer to? *That* (the subject) is singular; therefore, *is* (the verb) must also be singular as must be the quantifiers (*one*). What's the difference between a *step* and a *leap*? Now imagine you weren't reading this quote but hearing it. /ð/ represents the sound that "th" makes in the mouth. It's a voiced, interdental fricative phoneme, meaning the sound you make when you stick your tongue between your teeth, and vibrate your vocal cords continuously. This phoneme sounds very different from /s/ the sound that "s" makes. "Sat's a small step" would be understood completely differently. Then, there's the context. Who's saying this sentence? Where was it said? If a convicted felon had said this sentence when first entering a prison, it would have an entirely different meaning than Neil Armstrong landing on the moon. To complicate matters further, what Neil Armstrong meant to say was "That's one small step for [a] man..." Although the *a* was expunged, most cognizant English speakers readily understood the meaning of his words although the literal words differed significantly. And what's even more impressive is that from the time you first heard or read this quote and by the time you fully understood and interpreted all the implications of this quote, less than 5 seconds passed. Just looking at the figure below should give you some idea of how complicated understanding one sentence is:

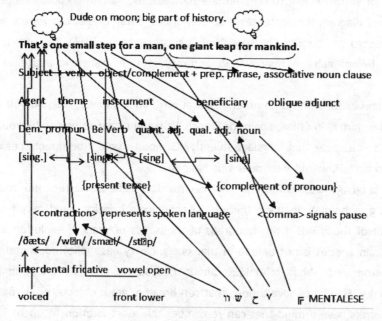

What's going on here? You've likely never heard the term "interdental fricative" before. You don't know the difference between a beneficiary and a theme. You've never spent more than a few seconds analyzing language in this kind of detail. And yet, you still understand the quote and can explain its meaning to others.

The secret to this riddle is why **you** have been hired to teach English to the Chinese although you may have never taught or studied English or linguistics before. You have **native** (or **near-native**) **English speaker credibility**. You were either born into or have spent significant time in an English-speaking environment and have internalized the "rules" of English communication. When you hear "That are one small steps ..." or "Sat's one small step ...,"

Chapter 2 What Is Language Teaching?

your mind instantly recognizes that something is wrong—a rule has been broken (even if you can't explain it as well as a linguistics professor could). In other words, your mind (if not you) already *knows* English much, much better than any student you will encounter during your time in China. But before you swell with pride, remember that innateness works against you, too. Native speakers of Chinese already know Chinese much, much better than you likely ever will.

Noam Chomsky, perhaps the most famous living linguist, talks about the **deep structure** that all languages possess. "Colorless green ideas sleep furiously," is the classic example of a literally meaningless English sentence that tricks the mind because it follows the meaningful **deep structure** of Englishgrammar. Lewis Carroll had intuited this underlying linguistic structure, aka deep structure, earlier when he wrote his "Jabberwocky" poem:

> Twas brillig, and the slithy toves
> Did gyre and gimble in the wabe:
> All mimsy were the borogoves,
> And the mome raths outgrabe.

Every non-impaired human mind innately acquires language. And all languages possess grammar (syntax, clauses, groups/phrases, words, morphemes), phonology (tone groups, foots, syllables, phonemes), and a pragmatic function (directness / ambiguity, formality / informality, cooperation / related principle, meaning). While all languages contain similar **deep structure**, the surface structures differ significantly. An analogy is computer hardware versus computer software. All computers contain similar hardware components to execute a similar function: a keyboard, a monitor, a hard drive, a mouse, etc. However, the software can differ significantly: Windows vs. Mac, MS Word vs. WordPerfect, Internet Explorer vs. Safari, etc. Likewise, meaning in one language can be conveyed in a second language very differently. If we were to directly translate "That's one small step for man, one giant leap for mankind" into other languages, it may be something like this:

> [Spanish] That is one step small for a man and one leap giant for mankind.
> [Chinese] One that be one and small step to one man, also one and giant step to man many.
> [Korean] For man, that one small step be [polite marker]. And, for people, that one giant leap be [polite marker].
> [Tagalog] It [sub. marker] step-one-small [obj. marker] for man-a [prep. marker] be [present-sing. marker], leap-one-giant [obj. marker] for mankind [prep marker].

What should be clear from the proceeding pages is that the human mind acquires any first language innately. However, acquiring a second language presents new difficulties, just as switching from Windows to Mac will take some time and a little instruction.

Language Acquisition Involves Hypotheses Testing and Deductive Reasoning

It would be impossible for children to hear every possible word, sentence, or combination of sounds that they are to reproduce in their lifetime. Yet, every single adult possesses the capability to create new sentences, ideas, and expressions that are readily by other speakers of that same language. This process occurs through a natural facility of the human mind known as deduction. Sherlock Holmes was a master of the deductive method. The detective eyes a smear of white paint on a suspect's shoe and "deduces" that this paint must correspond to the similar size and shape of missing paint on the door of the murder victim's apartment. I witness one Chinese student acing a math test, and my brain automatically deduces that all Chinese students are math wizzes. This entirely natural (if not laudatory) process is how the human mind works. We take the limited input we have and formulate a universal hypothesis.

This deductive process is apparent in children learning a language. They intuitively form hypotheses about the language they are learning and will use these hypotheses in their speech and writing until they are corrected. We can deduce what hypotheses they are testing through the errors they make when speaking. For example, a 4-year old may say, "Mommy, I jump-ed and jump-ed!" and then later, "I eated it all up!" What hypothesis is this child testing?

A 6-year old says, "Do you know why this water is cold? Because when it's frozened, it is stay cold a long time." A bad language teacher would simply correct the errors and have the student repeat after him or her. I want to challenge you to become a better language teacher. Think about what's taking place in this child's mind. What complex structures is the child applying? What simpler structures has the child not internalized? It's important to recognize that language learning involves grammatical rules (who, what, when, where matter); deductive hypotheses are constantly being tested. Children's mistakes are developmental and reflect learning. Compare these two examples:

"I eat it all up yesterday."
"I eated it all up yesterday."

Which child has made more progress in language acquisition?

2nd Language (L2) Acquisition v. 1st Language (L1) Acquisition

Let's begin using the acronyms **L1** for first language and **L2** for second language. It's important to recognize that like L1 learners, L2 learners:

- Form hypotheses about the language they are learning.
- Do not necessarily acquire language structures in an order we expect.
- Make mistakes that are developmental and reflect learning.

Think about when you first began studying your L2. More likely than not, you would read or hear the sentence in the second L2, and then immediately translate it directly into your L1. Vice-

Chapter 2 What Is Language Teaching?

versa, whenever you wanted to speak or write in your L2, you would have to first think in your L1 and then directly translate it into the L2. This is a phenomenon known as **transference** and occurs naturally in all humans whose L1 is stronger than their L2.

Sometimes transference works in your favor; other times it does not. **Positive transference** occurs when the L1 and L2 are similar. The learner directly transfers syntactical knowledge from her L1 to produce similarly correct forms in the L2. For example, Spanish speakers learning French quickly acquire the idea of feminine and masculine articles (*le, la*) because Spanish contains similar structures (el, la). Negative transference, or **interference**, occurs when the L1 and L2 have differing structures. For example, Chinese learners of English struggle with articles (*a, an, the*) because no corresponding structure for articles exists in Chinese. Likewise, you'll often hear Chinese speakers call girls, "he," and men, "she." This is because the word *ta* in Chinese translates directly to *he* or *she*.

The two types of errors L2 learners will make can be categorized as either:

- **Interlanguage errors**—caused by interference from the 1st language, or
- **Intralanguage errors**—caused by inconsistencies in the 2nd language

Interlanguage Errors

L2 learners may be helped or hindered by interference from their first language.

- **Negative transference** or **interference**: Learner uses 1st language structure, resulting in an error in the 2nd language.
- **Positive transference**: Learner uses 1st language structure, resulting in a correct form in the 2nd language.

Look at the following sentence spoken by a native Spanish-speaker learning English:

"I have a pen blue."

1. What negative transfer from the L1 (Spanish) to the L2 (English) is occurring?
2. What positive transfer from the L1 (Spanish) to the L2 (English) is occurring?

Native Chinese speakers learning English will tend to make the following interlanguage errors:

1) Confusing gender pronouns (he, she)
2) Forgetting articles (the, a, an)
3) Forgetting to add "s" to make words plural
4) Pronunciation of "th", "r" vs. "l"

The reason why these errors commonly occur among Chinese learners of English is simple: these grammatical structures do not exist in Chinese! *Ta* in Chinese means both *he* and *she*. Chinese employs a very different article system for countable nouns. Rather than adding -s to the make words plural, Chinese uses -men. /r/ and /l/ are not phonetically differentiated in Chinese.

And the /ð/ phoneme does not appear in Chinese pronunciation. Thus, we can predict that where grammatical structures differ between the 1st and 2nd language, negative transference and errors are more likely to occur.

Intralanguage Errors

Look at the following sentence spoken by a learner of English:

"Yesterday I goed to dinner with my friends and we ate steak."

What intralanguage error is being made?

We can predict what errors our students will face based on knowledge of both their native language and the target language. Knowledge of students' native language helps predict interlanguage errors. Knowledge of the target language helps predict intralanguage errors. Native Chinese speakers learning English will tend to make the following intralanguage errors:

1) Past-tense endings and irregular verbs
2) Forming questions with "Do"
3) Prepositions
4) Forgetting to add "s" to third-person singular verbs (She walks.)

It's important to note that young children learning English as their first language will also make several of these same errors. This is because learning a language is tough, irregularities are frequent, and, especially in English, "rules" are often vaguer than English teachers would like. For example, how would teach a six year old the difference between *of* and *for*? If you can answer that question succinctly, several linguistics professors would like to talk with you.

Affective Filters

Differences and similarities between the learner's L1 and L2 are not the only factors that determine the ease and speed with which the new language will be acquired. Personality and subconscious objectives for learning a second language can affect the efficacy of learning. If a student is not in the mood to learn or views the second language and culture negatively, little learning is likely to take place. Similarly, if a student lacks intrinsic or extrinsic motivation to learn a language or fails to set goals for their learning, then a strong filter arises, which will negatively affect the student's L2 acquisition.

In a group of 3~4, discuss the following questions:

1. What do you anticipate as positive affective filters your students will have toward learning English?
2. What do you anticipate as negative affective filters your students will have toward learning English?

When we talk about **motivation**, we need to separate **extrinsic** from **intrinsic** motivation. Extrinsic motivation comes from outside the learner, for example: a pat on the back, a smile from the teacher, or an A grade on a test. Intrinsic motivation comes from within the learner, for example: an interest in foreign cultures, a desire to communicate with people from other countries, or a want for a better life.

Personality can also greatly affect individual learners' L2 acquisition. Students may be generally classified into one of two groups: *extroverts,* who learn better through interaction with other learners and language speakers; and introverts, who learn better through reading, listening, and interacting one-on-one.

Return to the same group as before, and discuss the following questions:

1. Which type of motivation do you think is stronger for most language learners?
2. As a teacher, how can you increase extrinsic motivation?
3. As a teacher, how can you increase intrinsic motivation?
4. As a teacher how can you accommodate both types of learning personalities?

Reflection and Activity for Teachers

1. Why do children overgeneralize new language structures in their L1, as in the example of the past -ed (taked)?
2. Reflect on a foreign language you have learned and write down a few interlanguage errors you have typically made (i.e, mistakes caused by the interference of your 1st language). Discuss these with a partner.
3. Chinese students of English often have trouble with articles and the plural "s". As an English teacher in China, how might you help your students master these two difficult areas of English?
4. What can you do to be sure that both extroverted and introverted students are actively involved in the learning process?
5. How do you think you can inspire intrinsic motivation among your students? How can you make activities more interesting to your students?

English 2.011

Whenever someone ignorant of language asks me why kids these days can't speak or write proper English, my reply is, "What is proper English? Is it Shakespeare's English? Chaucer's English? Modern-day Australian English? 18th-century Bostonian English? Southern African-American vernacular English?" The truth is that the English that we read and hear every day is just the latest software update, English 2.011 if you will. While all humans possess the same linguistic hardware (innate brain centers for language, teeth, tongues, lips, vocal cords, ears, etc.), the software (language itself) can differ dramatically. Moreover, due to the widespread nature of

English in particular, multiple software versions of "proper" English exist throughout the world. Would you ever tell a native English speaker from England to speak "proper" English like an American? Would you tell a Latino-American to speak English with a "proper", white accent? Hopefully not, but many English teachers will unblushingly criticize their students' writing and speech when it does not conform to their idea of "proper" English (the version that they were taught). A quick history of the English language will point out the fallacy of viewing any language as a universal, unchanging constant that can be standardized to any one person's idea of what is and what is not "proper."

- No English is spoken until the 8th century.
- Vikings invade Anglo-Saxons in the 8th century; Old English (see Beowulf) is created from the creolization of Germanic, Anglo-Saxon, and Latin languages.
- Norman Conquest of 1066—1400, Latin, French, and English were spoken in that order.
- Middle English (see Chaucer) during this period came from Norman French, Parisian French, and Scandinavian.
- From 1450—1700 the Great Vowel Shift occurs. English speakers begin to imitate the vowel sounds of French, the language of the aristocracy at the time.
- 1700—1800. Certain words and structures disappear; new words are created or borrowed from other languages. For example, *thou*, *thine*, and *you is* are no longer in common use. *Kimono, patio, sauerkraut* are accepted as common English.
- English expands to the Americas, Australia, South Africa, etc. Various dialects and sub-dialects appear; for example, African-American Vernacular English (AAVE), Latino English, Bostonian English, South Park English, Standard American Academic English.
- Webster's Dictionary and governmental policies on language education attempt to formalize "proper" English.
- Today, many believe that globalization and mass media are leading to a re-homogenization of English and many are taught that "proper" English is newscaster English.

To me, language is the ultimate proof for Darwin's theory of evolution. Languages are constantly replicating and mutating. Some mutations adapt well to changes in the environment (e.g., slang like *cool* and *hot* are still nearly universally accepted and repeated by speakers of English); other mutations do not adapt well to changes in the environment and quickly die off (e.g., *groovy* and *square*). In fact, new languages (like English in the 8th century) are created continually through the replication and mutation that occurs when two different languages come into contact.

Chapter 2 What Is Language Teaching?

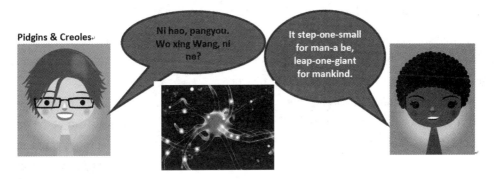

!!!Software does not compute! Must create new language!!!

A **pidgin** is a simplified language that develops when two or more groups that do not share a common language are required to communicate. For example, your students may laughingly refer to themselves as speakers of Chinglish, a simplified hybrid of Chinese and English wherein some basic English words are superimposed onto the grammatical structures inherent in Chinese. If this **pidgin** is repeated and formally accepted as meaningful, it may be passed down to future generations as their 1st language. Once a pidgin language becomes the native and primary language of children, it is known as a **creole.** Viking invaders in the 8th century mixed with the Anglo-Saxons to create a **pidgin**, which was consequently accepted and passed down to future generations to create a **creole** we know as the English language. Throughout the entire process of language creation, replication and mutation (i.e., evolution) are the driving forces.

Some Language Learning Theories Are Unsound

Mark Twain once wrote,"It ain't what you do know that gets you in trouble. It's what you know that ain't so." This is no truer than in the field of language learning. Old wives' tales about where language comes from and how it is acquired abound today, despite ample scientific research that easily disproves such theories. Here's a few of the most prevalent unsound theories and their deleterious effects on students' learning:

1. **Connectionism**—we learn a language by making connections to the language we previously learned. For example, we have first learned the word *bird*. Then, we encounter new words we connect them in relation to this word: bird ←→ fly ←→ wing ←→ airplane ←→ migrate ←→ warm-blooded ←→ mammal ← mouth → beak ←→ regurgitate ←→ nest. Eventually, the connections expand and overlap to create a neural network of images in our mind, so that when we read or hear a word it triggers the nearby connections in our minds and thus is language acquired. Unfortunately, this theory cannot be entirely true. Otherwise, these sentences would all be equivalent:

    a. That's one small step for mankind, one giant leap for a man.
    b. One giant leap a man, that's a small step for one mankind.
    c. That's a small man, leap one giant, a step of one mankind.

d. Mankind one giant leap, that's for a one small man step.

Our mind instantly recognizes that language is more than just a group of words connected together. The order, or **syntax**, of those words makes an important difference. Therefore, the connectionism theory cannot be the entire answer.

The resulting pedagogy of teachers who follow this unsound theory often appears as unstructured, unfocused group discussion. "Just keep talking," "Language can't be taught," "The only way to learn a language is to practice it and absorb it," are platitudes these teachers repeatedly declare without any logical examination. As we've already seen, acquiring an L1 is much different than acquiring an L2. Students may lack the vocabulary to just keep talking. They may keep talking, but without a great deal of accuracy or complexity. Students are likely uncertain what aspects of the L2 require more practice and which they have already mastered. Plus, they may not recognize when they mistakes and where the L2 differs from their L1. In other words, L2 acquisition can—and should—be taught. The brain doesn't automatically acquire an L2 through osmosis and connectionism.

2. **Tabla Rasa** (The Blank Slate)—children are born into the world with no innate structures, and are purely a product of their environments. Therefore, children must be explicitly taught by their guardians, teachers, and community how to speak. There are several proofs which nullify this theory.

1. Parents would have to be strict linguistics professors with complete knowledge of the language for their children to speak so fluently and accurately and such a young age. Obviously, most parents could never explicitly teach language to their children.
2. All children, regardless of environment, learn to speak fluently and accurately at a relatively young age. They also pass through a naturally-occuring **critical period** (age 3-6), during which their linguistic production grows at a quantum rate.
3. Children would not apply grammar rules to words no adult would ever have taught them (e.g. He hitted me. We drived to her house.)

The resulting pedagogy from teachers who follow this unsound theory often appears as teacher-led, accuracy based. "Repeat after me," "That's not proper English," "Listen to how I say it," are instructions these teachers repeatedly offer their students. But there is no one way to speak or write. Language is constantly evolving and students have their own ideas and styles of communication. Tabla Rasa teaching drains the natural energy and interest students have for language study and self-expression. Plus, while the drills may be memorized for a short time and regurgitated back on tests, in the long run the language is forgotten and not acquired due to lack of authentic practice.

3. **Mimicry**—we learn a language by listening, absorbing, and parroting back what we hear. This cannot be true because:

1. We recognize that stutters, fillers (uhm, oh, well), coughs and hiccups are not meaningful to communication and do not attempt to mimic them in our speech.
2. If all language were simple mimicry, new ideas could never be created. In his short story

Chapter 2 What Is Language Teaching?

"The Library of Babel," Jorge Louis Borges describes an infinite universe of books, all containing the same number of pages and letters, but which all differ from the others although in some cases only by one letter. While this may be an exaggeration, no sane person would doubt the **combinatorial power** of language to create novel expression. For example, you may have heard before that Neil Armstrong declared, "That's one small step for man, one giant leap for mankind," when first landing on the moon. However, have your ever heard or read these novel expressions?

- Neil Armstrong declared, "That's one small step for man, one giant leap for mankind" in a Hollywood studio.
- The TEFL teacher wrote that Neil Armstrong declared, "That's one small step for man, one giant leap for mankind," in a Hollywood studio.
- In a Hollywood studio, Neil Armstrong declared, "That's one small step for man, one giant leap for mankind" is what I read that the TEFL teacher wrote.

The problem with all these unsound theories for language acquisition is that they attempt to alter something so complicated and big into one, single, small explanation. Yes, true language acquisition does involve connecting new vocabulary to previous vocabulary. Yes, it is true that one's environment significantly affects how language is acquired. Yes, humans do mimic others' speech and words. But, true language acquisition is all these things and more. True language acquisition includes creativity of expression through the combinatorial powers of language. It includes the beautiful evolution of a human mind naturally selected over thousands of millions of years to prize language and form innate structures in the brain. These structures enable individuals to acquire any language on Earth faster and more effectively than even the best language teacher could ever hope to accomplish.

CTLC leader James Swihart (formal US ambassador to Ethiopia) at the Foreign Expert Bureau Recruiting Conference in China
CTLC 负责人在国家外专局外教招聘会上

Lesson Planning

Chapter 3

The goals for this chapter are:
- To be able to assess the level of your students.
- To create lesson plans for your first day of class.
- To develop lesson planning skills that build step-by-step toward your students' goals.

Formal Lesson Plan

- Level:
- Language Objective:
- Skills Focus:
- Estimated Time:
  1. Warm-Up Activity:
  2. Activity 1:
  3. Class-Discussion/Reflection/Summary:
  4. Activity 2:
  5. Conclusion
  6. Extension
- Materials Needed:
- Assessment:

Chapter 3 Lesson Planning

Level

TEFL classes in China are typically divided by age. 1st graders are 6 year-olds. 6th graders are 11—13 year-olds. High school seniors are 17—18 year-olds.

By now, you should realize that language acquisition has little direct correlation to a student's age. There are other ways to assess a student's L2 level. Can you think of some ways to test your students' English level? (We'll cover assessment in greater detail in a future chapter.)

1. Tests for Fluency
   a.
   b.
2. Tests for Accuracy
   a.
   b.
3. Tests for Complexity
   a.
   b.

Language Objective

Every teaching lesson plan should have an objective. For ESOL lesson plans, the primary objective will be for your students—NOT YOU—to improve *their* English speaking, listening, reading, or writing skills.

> **Law One: There is a difference between teaching and performing.**
> **You are not an entertainer! You are a teacher.**

Now that you have determined your class' **level**, you can begin to focus on what the language objective for the lesson will be. **Listening, speaking, reading,** and **writing** are considered to be the **four basic divisions of language teaching**. They are also a good place to start determining what the **language objective** for your lesson will be.

■ Language Objective: Speaking/Listening: furniture names

> **Law Two: Good lesson plans extend the previous lesson plans.**

The objective for new lessons should build upon objectives from old lessons. Much like a new construction is built upon a solid scaffold, **scaffolding** describes the process by which new knowledge is built upon existing knowledge. You can ask your students what they have already learned. You can ask your *colleagues* (yes you are now someone's colleague). Your students may or may not use a textbook with weekly language objectives. For example, last week the main objective of your lessons was for students to learn the names of different furniture. Today, you **extend the previous lesson**, and evolve the language objective to describing locations of different furniture (e.g., behind the sofa, under the table, to the left of the desk). Next week, you could further **extend the lesson** to using furniture to give directions (e.g., walk to the desk, turn right at the sofa, and look below the chair).

■ Language Objective: Speaking/listening: furniture names + directions.

Law Three: Specific language objectives make your teaching better and your students' **learning easier.**

"What are we learning today?" the students ask me. I need to be able to answer this most important question. We are learning X X X or (1), (2), (3). Many organized teachers outline the day's lesson on the whiteboard. I cannot recommend enough for new teachers to write on the board at the start of each class: "Today we will learn:

1.
2.
3.

Organization is a key part of effective teaching. By adding **detail** to your rough **language objective(s)**, you can begin to break down the lesson. You can begin to consider the methods you will use in your teaching. Do you want to focus on students' **fluency**, **accuracy**, **complexity**? How will students demonstrate their acquisition of the lesson? Are your expectations for students acquiring the language objective realistic? How will you measure whether or not your students have acquired the language objective? Take a deep breath. Think like a teacher. Yes. Slow down. Be professional. Think in advance. Get organized.

Of all the elements in the formal lesson (do you remember what they are?) **language**

objectives are most worthy to a new teacher's time spent in preparation. Pay careful attention to the example below.

- Language Objective: Speaking/listening + accuracy: furniture names + directions.

    By the end of today's lessons, students will have learned:

    1) The names of common furniture—sofa, chair, bed, desk, table, window, microwave, trash can, computer, door, oven, and dishwasher.

    2) How to give and understand basic directions—turn to the left/right, look below/above, go forward/back/1/2/3/4 steps, across from, next to, far/near.

    3) How to ask for and give accurate directions in the form of complete sentences.

Reflection and Activity for Teachers

1. Imagine you are teaching a 6th grade class. Last week, they studied geography and the names of some countries where English is spoken (USA, UK, Pakistan, New Zealand, Australia, Canada, Ireland, Uganda, South Africa, Philippines, India). Write a specific language objective.
2. Share your specific language objectives with your group.

Skills Focus

There are other aspects to learning a language beyond the literal words and grammar. Examples of possible TEFL skills focus-based lesson plans include:

1. Timed speaking/writing (speaking/writing faster/longer)
2. Introductions
3. Politeness strategies
4. Asking follow-up questions
5. Learn to mingle
6. Gestures
7. Chit-chat/small talk
8. Interviews
9. Telephone calls
10. Changing the topic
11. Group discussion
12. Debates

Can you think of a few more?
Don't worry, we'll see several examples of skills focus in the chapters to come.

Estimated Time

Pacing is another essential to teaching. "How long should an activity last?" "How many activities do I need for one class?" "What do if the activity is taking longer than I anticipated?" "What if the students finish the activity early?" These are some of the most common questions new teachers ask their more experienced colleagues. This is one of many reasons why this TEFL Training in China Program was created.

Tip 1: TEFL teachers always wear a watch.

Tip 2: TEFL teachers estimate the time required for each component of a lesson plan.

Tip 3: TEFL teachers record and evaluate successful lesson plans according to time.

Notice that **level** plays a large role in determining the **estimated time** for a lesson plan. With advanced-level TEFL classes, activities expected to last ten minutes can run on and on because the students possess the linguistic capabilities to speak, question, and initiate discussion. For low-level classes, activities expected to last ten minutes can die out after three because the students do not possess the linguistic capabilities needed. This may sound like a cop out, but **pacing** really is a matter of experience. As a new teacher, you'll quickly develop your own sense of timing. And it's important to realize that each teacher is different, especially when it comes to **pacing**. For now, just realize that:

Tip 4: TEFL teachers recognize ebbs and flows in the lesson.

Tip 5: TEFL teachers know how to begin and end a class.

➢ Alternate brisk, high-energy activities with slower, thoughtful activities.

➢ Follow a teacher-fronted activity with one involving pairs or small groups.

➢ Follow individual silent reading with verbal pair work based on the reading.

➢ If they have been working on something very challenging, give them something lighter.

Please note that every class is different and every lesson plan is different. However, there are some general timing patterns that experienced TEFL teachers will follow based upon the class level and the language or skill objective. Always prepare more than you anticipate will be necessary. You can always save leftover material for the next class. Also, don't be afraid to scrap a lesson plan that isn't working and use an alternative or Lesson Plan B. Here are a few generic lesson plans with estimated times for various levels and objectives:

- Level: Low, 3rd grade
- Language Objective: Speaking + building vocabulary + increasing fluency
- Skills Focus: Speaking complete sentences
- Estimated Time: 50 minutes

  1. Warm-up activity (3 ~ 5 min.)

  2. Introduction of today's language objective/skills focus, teacher models correct use (3 ~ 5 min.)

  3. Teacher practices the language objective/skill focus with the class (5 ~ 10 min.)

  4. Activity #1: Pair work/small group activity (5 min.)

  5. Review/students make corrections (5 min.)

  6. Activity #2: Draw a picture/sing a song/game (5 ~ 10 min.)

7. Review/students make corrections (5 min.)
8. Activity #3: TPR/workbook exercise (5 min.)
9. Review/students make corrections (5 min.)
10. Activity #4: Game/song/TPR (5 min.)
11. Students summarize/review the lesson (2 ~ 3 min.)

- Level: Intermediate, 7th grade
- Language Objective: Speaking + Past tense regular verbs + accuracy
- Skills Focus: Speaking complete sentences + asking/answering questions
- Estimated Time: 50 minutes
    1. Warm-up activity (3 ~ 5 min.)
    2. Introduction of today's language objective/skills focus, teacher models correct use (1 ~ 2 min.)
    3. Teacher practices the language objective/skill focus with the class (2 ~ 3 min.)
    4. Activity #1: Pair work/small group activity (10 ~ 15 min.)
    5. Review/students make corrections (5 min.)
    6. Activity #2: Role play/sing a song/game (5 ~ 15 min.)
    7. Review/students make correction (5 min.)
    8. Activity #3: workbook exercise (5 ~ 10 min.)
    9. Students summarize/review the lesson (5 ~ 10 min.)

- Level: Advanced, 11th grade
- Language Objective: Speaking + complex sentences
- Skills Focus: debate + logical reasoning + argumentative support
- Estimated Time: 50 minutes
    1. Warm-up activity (3 ~ 5 min.)
    2. Introduction of today's language objective/skills focus, teacher models correct use (1 ~ 2 min.)
    3. Teacher practices the language objective/skill focus with the class (2 ~ 3 min.)
    4. Activity #1: Students debate (30 ~ 40 min.)
    5. Students summarize/review the lesson (5 ~ 10 min.)

Reflection and Activity for Teachers

1. Create two lesson plans. Estimate the time for each component of your plan.
2. Share your lessons plans with your group. Do you agree with the time estimates?
3. Imagine you are teaching a low-level 3rd grade class. The language objective of your lesson plan is names of food, but your lesson plan only covers the first 20-minutes of a 50-minute class. How could extend the lesson for the next 30 minutes and maintain your professionalism?

Designing Activities that Match Language Objectives and/or Skills Foci

The best activities are the ones that connect to your language objective and/or skills foci. In other words, an effective activity actually improves students' knowledge and use of the target language. So many new teachers fall in the trap of playing games with their students rather than teaching them a language. Do not fall into this trap, or you will make your TEFL trainer look bad! Rule #1 of Teaching: Don't make your teacher look bad! In order for the teacher to look good, students: (a) need to enjoy the class and (b) demonstrate improvement in their English. Students often leave the classroom smiling and happy, but ultimately uneducated in the target language. This may be good babysitting or gamesmanship, but it is not good teaching. When designing activities, it may help to visually map activities around your lesson goal:

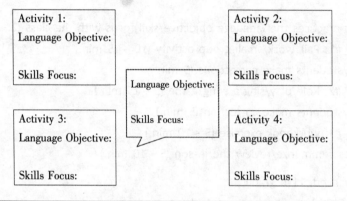

Reflection and Activity for Teachers

1. Review your lesson plans from this chapter. How do the activities in your lessons connect to the language objective or skills focus for the lesson?
2. A warm-up activity creates interest in the lesson. What are same ways to create interest at the start of class?
3. Apply scaffolding to extend one of today's lesson plans into tomorrow's lesson plan.

Adapting and Revising Lesson Plans

Chapter 4

The goals for this chapter are:
- To assess published lesson plans.
- To learn how to adapt and revise others' lesson plans to fit the needs of YOUR students.

Adapting and Revising Lessons Plans

The sample lesson plans provided in this chapter have worked in other teachers' classrooms but may not necessarily work in yours. We teach students who have individual preferences and styles of language learning. An effective lesson plan is geared toward a particular audience. Therefore, you should carefully consider how to adapt and revise published lessons plans to make them your own. As Picasso said, "Good artists copy and great artists steal." As you read the first sample lesson, Jobs, consider how you could revise the plan to make it more interesting and personally meaningful to your students.

Lesson for Revision: Jobs

Level : Pre-intermediate
Language Focus : Vocabulary
Skills Focus : Comparing/contrasting different jobs

Warm-Up Activity: Q&A about jobs

The teacher writes a list of different jobs on the board (receptionist, lawyer, taxi driver, musician, etc.). The teacher then asks the class if they ever thought of applying for jobs in the future. Next, the teacher makes a check by each job that interests any of the students.

Activity 1: Class discussion

The class is asked if they think the jobs checked on the board are considered good jobs in their home country or not. The teacher then leads a discussion on whether it is difficult or not to get a good job in China.

Activity 2: Writing exercise

The class is told to imagine they are being interviewed for an important job. Individually, students write a list of questions that interviewers typically ask candidates (Did you graduate from university? What was your major? Were you involved in any extra-curricular activities?), which the teacher has already listed on the board for them. The students exchange questions and answer their partners' questions.

Activity 3: Class discussion

The class talks about the interviews. Students are called on in alphabetical order to read their interview questions and answers.

Reflection and Activity for Teachers

1. How can this lesson plan be made more communicative? How can each and every student simultaneously practice speaking and listening?
2. Do you think this lesson is appropriately geared to the stated level (pre-intermediate)? If not, what revisions could you make to better suit the lesson to the intended level?
3. The teacher has forgotten to consider the closure to this lesson. How would you end this lesson plan?

Task-Based Lessons

Task based lessons usually involve students working in small groups to achieve an authentic, open-ended, but specific chore which promotes communication in the target language.

Task-Based Lesson 1: Time Capsule

Level: Beginner +

Language Focus: Vocabulary

Skills Focus: Speaking practice, collaboration, making decisions

Warm-Up Activity: Quick write

Tell the class they have five minutes to write down as many items as they can that will be different in the world 100 years from now. After they've compiled their lists, elicit a few answers from random students.

Activity 1: Small group activity

In groups of four to six students, tell the class that each group is going to bury a box in the group for future generations to find. This box will contain seven items or photos of objects which will tell people in the future about life in their country and the world in the current year. Groups discuss and eventually decide as a group what will go into the time capsule.

Activity 2: Class discussion

Have each group report to the class on the items they chose to put into the time capsule and why they selected those particular items. Students should be encouraged to elaborate on their choices. The teacher can facilitate the discussion by asking, "What will the item (e.g., an MP3 player) tell people of the future about how the world was in our time?" or "What do you think people of the future will think about this item?"

Reflection and Activity for Teachers

1. Name three things you like about this lesson plan. Name three things you dislike.
2. How would you revise and adapt this lesson plan for an intermediate-level class? Support your changes.

Task-Based Lesson 2: Planning an Itinerary

Level: Beginner +
Language Focus: Vocabulary, transition words: first, then, after, later, finally
Skills Focus: Speaking fluency, collaboration, making decisions

Warm-Up Activity: Class discussion

Ask the class if anyone has ever received a guest from another country. If no one has, then ask if someone has received visitors from another part of China or use yourself as an example. Discuss what the responding students took their guests to see in their hometown: a museum, park, concert, favorite restaurant, etc.

Activity 1: Small group activity

Divide the class in groups of four or six. Explain to each group that a group of American teenagers are coming to visit their hometown for one week to learn about life in China, but they have no itinerary. (You may have to explain what itinerary means or model one for your students). It is the group's job to plan a list of interesting and fun things to do for one week. Events could include going to a concert, visiting a school, or having a meal with a family. You should emphasize that the visiting teenagers are coming to your hometown to learn as much as possible about life in China, so the events selected should reflect typical and interesting aspects of China. (Don't forget to circulate to check that everyone is on task and speaking in English!)

Activity 2: Class discussion

Someone from each group (or selected groups if the class is large) reads their group's list of events and talks about why they chose those events. Write all the lists on the board, and after all the groups have finished, have the class vote on a combined list of the top ten things to do while visiting China. Finally, erase the superfluous events and write a top ten list on the board.

> **Reflection and Activity for Teachers**
>
> 1. Class discussions in large classes have a tendency to become teacher-centered (i.e., teacher asks the question to one student; he/she gives a short response; and the teacher elaborates and writes a summary on the board). How could you make the class discussions in this lesson more student-centered?
> 2. The lesson plans fails to provide closure or consideration for the next week's lesson. How could you end this lesson and begin to extend the acquired language and skills into the next lesson plan?

Task-Based Lesson 3: The Titanic is Sinking!

This is a problem-solving lesson which engages the class in activities that promote teamwork, decision-making, and cooperation. Problem-solving activities engage students in group work requiring collaborative decision-making, and therefore, are very effective in large communicative-based classes.

Level : Pre-intermediate +

Language Focus : Vocabulary for professions

Skills Focus : Speaking and listening practice, collaborative decision-making

Warm-Up Activity : Eliciting vocabulary

The teacher asks if anyone has ever seen the movie *Titanic*, then comments briefly on the film. Next, a list of professions is elicited (at least 20, such as lawyer, doctor, musician, etc.) from the class and these are written on the board as the students call them out. The teacher then adds *old lady*, *pregnant woman*, and *little child* to the list.

Activity 1: Group discussion

Students get into groups of four. It is explained to the class that the Titanic is sinking and there is only room to save five passengers. Each group discusses, decides, and jots down which five people they will save and why.

Activity 2: Teacher-centered Q&A

A representative from each group is called on to read their group's list of people to be saved and explains why just these people were chosen.

Activity 3: Class discussion

Finally, the whole class votes on five people to save while you tally the votes on the

Chapter 4 Adapting and Revising Lesson Plans

board next to each passenger and indicate which final five people have been chosen to be saved.

> **Reflection and Activity for Teachers**
> 1. Your class is slightly more advanced and finds this lesson to simple. How could you adapt this lesson to a higher-level class and introduce more advanced language and skills foci?
> 2. Your students look tired and have been sitting in groups around a table for the past few lessons. How could you incorporate more physical and interpersonal intelligences into the activity?

Content-Based Lesson Plans

Content- or theme-based lesson plans center around a topic of interest to students.

Content-Based Lesson Plan 1: The American Dream

Level: Intermediate +

Language Focus: New and familiar vocabulary

Skills Focus: Reading practice, speaking practice, collaborative paraphrasing, and critical thinking

Materials: Excerpt from Martin Luther King's "I Have a Dream"

Warm-Up Activity: Q&A

Write *The American Dream* on the board and ask the class, "Have you ever heard of the American Dream? What do you think this could be?" Elicit a few random responses. If no one responds, prompt the class by asking, "Is it to have a big house? What do you think?"

Activity 1: Group work

Each pair joins another pair to make groups of four while you hand out excerpts from Dr. King's speech (see next page). The groups are given a few minutes to read through the text and ask about new vocabulary. (Be prepared to define a number of words and write them on the board: manacles, segregation, languished, etc.). Next, groups discuss possible answers to the following two questions: (1) What is Dr. King's message? (2) What is Dr. King's American dream?

Activity 2: Teacher-fronted Q&A

Speakers from several of the groups are called on to read their answers to the rest of the class while you list the descriptions on the board and draw attention to similarities between the previous list on the board and the students' ideas.

Activity 3: Class discussion

The class discusses *The Chinese Dream*. "Is there a Chinese dream? What is the Chinese dream? How is it different from the American dream? How is similar?"

Activity 4: Cool-down

Time permitting, students write a page about their own personal dreams and aspirations for the future. "What would you like to do when you finish high school? After college?" (A good warm-up activity to start the subsequent lesson involves having students write about their personal aspirations and then share or present these to the rest of the class).

Excerpt from Dr. Martin Luther King's "I Have a Dream" speech:

One hundred years later, the Negro still is not free. One hundred years later, the life of the Negro is still sadly crippled by the manacles of segregation and the chains of discrimination. One hundred years later, the Negro lives on a lonely island of poverty in the midst of a vast ocean of material prosperity. One hundred years later, the Negro is still languished in the corners of American society and finds himself an exile in his own land...

...I say to you, my friends, that even though we must face the difficulties of today and tomorrow, I still have a dream. It is a dream deeply rooted in the American Dream that one day this nation will rise up and live out the true meaning of its creed - we hold these truths to be self-evident, that all men are created equal.

Reflection and Activity for Teachers

1. How do you feel about using literary material in your teaching? Do you think it would serve as a useful prompt for discussions?
2. Do you think the above excerpt will be level-appropriate for your students? If not, how could you adapt this excerpt to meet the level of your students?
3. How do you feel about challenging your students to criticize culture and historical dreams as in this lesson?

Communicative Lessons

We've already discussed CLT. The primary goal for communicative lessons is to get your students to talk as much as possible. Normally, the focus of communicative lessons is on fluency rather than accuracy.

Communicative Lesson 1: Introductions

Level: Beginner +

Language Focus: Vocabulary, questions

Skills Focus: Speaking practice

This is a fairly detailed "getting to know you" plan designed for the first or second class of a new course. It provides a good opportunity for speaking practice and a chance for you and

Chapter 4 Adapting and Revising Lesson Plans

your students to get to know each other. So, start right off by having them ask you questions in order to get to know you. Getting to know your students and taking a personal interest in them will help to build all-important rapport between you and them, and will keep them on your side on those days when your lessons don't go as planned.

Warm-Up Activity : Guess about me

Ideally, this game is done on power point presentation. Alternatively, you can draw pictures on the board of things that represent you and your life (e.g., photos your family, a map of your hometown, your favorite sport, hobby, etc.). Prior to the lesson, you should spend some time thinking about what images you will use to represent yourself to your class.

For example, draw a rough outline of the U.S. and a tennis racket and have the class ask questions related to the image you have drawn.

Student A: Are you from the United States?

Student B: Do you play tennis?

And so on. You could also bring some objects to class that represent your interests. Let students ask you the names of the objects if they don't know them, and ask you some questions about them. For example, if you bring a soccer ball, they might ask how often you play, if you play on a team, what position you play, etc.

Activity 1: Pair work

On the board, the teacher writes a few questions about the students' names: Does your name have a meaning? Why did your parents choose your name? Do you have a nickname? (Explain the meaning of nickname and tell the class something about your nickname if you have one). Do you like your name?

Students get into pairs, copy the questions from the board, and take turns interviewing each other about their names. Interviewers should write down their respondent's answers.

Partners take turns introducing each other to the rest of the class and read their partner's answers to the class. (Don't forget to circulate to check that everyone is working on the activity and speaking English!)

Activity 2: Individual writing

Write a letter to your students the evening before your class. Include in the letter as much personal information about yourself as you feel comfortable sharing (see sample letter below). Hand out copies of your letter to all students. If a copier is not available, you can dictate the letter to the class. Give the class a few minutes to read your letter. Check comprehension.

Then, students each write a letter to you in reply to your letter. Next, have students stand up one at a time to read their letter in front of the class. Comment on the letters as you like, frequently providing encouragement. With larger class, you can select a number of students (10—15) to read their letters.

Sample Letter

Dear Students,

My name is John and I have come to China in order to learn about Chinese culture and to meet many Chinese people. I am trying to learn the Chinese language, but it's not easy. Last year, I graduated from the University of Wisconsin with a degree in cultural anthropology. In my free time, I like to play piano. I love Chinese food, and my favorite dish is Peking Duck. I'm looking forward to teaching English in China because I think a lot of interesting things can happen in a classroom. People get to know each other and share a lot of ideas. I'm glad that you are in this class. Please write me about yourself.

Sincerely,
John

Reflection and Activity for Teachers

1. Do you think this plan is effective in reaching its stated goal in helping students and the teacher get to know each other? Explain.
2. How could you adapt these activities if your students are unable to correctly formulate questions in English? Would modeling work in this case?
3. How could you adapt this plan so that shy students would not be embarrassed to speak aloud when called upon?

Communicative Lesson 2: Debating

Not only do debates enable students to engage in affective-based discussions in the target language, but they also promote critical thinking and the expression of personal viewpoints.

Level : Intermediate +

Language Focus : New and familiar vocabulary, persuasive and argumentative phrases

Skills Focus : Reading practice, developing and defending an argument

Materials : Write a list of five debatable statements on the board before class begins. Examples might include: school summer breaks should be longer, women are better drivers than men, clean air is more important than developing industry, remaining with your family is more important than moving to another city to find a job, animals shouldn't be kept in zoos, etc. Better yet is to use controversial statements from your students or interests from previous class discussions.

Warm-Up Activity : Debates

Write the word debate on the board and ask the class if they can tell you the meaning. "What's the difference between debate, discussion, and fighting? Have you ever had a debate before? When? Where? In school?" Then, explain that today there will be a debate.

Activity 1: Group discussion

Divide the class into groups of five or seven. Each group discusses and debates whether they, as a group, agree or disagree with the statements. They must reach a consensus within their group. As with all small group or pair work activities, be sure to circulate around the room to check that the groups are engaged in the activity, make suggestions, comments, or play devil's advocate as you like.

Activity 2: Class discussion

Call one person from a group to stand and read aloud the first statement. Then, ask whether the group agreed with it or not, and why. Next, ask if the other groups are in agreement with the group that has just answered. If there is a dissenting group, then that group must try to defend itself by having one group member stand up and explain their group's point of view. The debate on a given topic could go on for a few minutes but should be limited to allow other groups a chance to talk. Continue the round-robin debate on the remaining topics.

Reflection and Activity for Teachers

1. How could you adapt this lesson for a shy class that might view debating as a verbal conflict in which one party eventually loses face?
2. Imagine that several of the groups reach a quick consensus on the five statements and begin to revert to speaking in Chinese. As you walk by and implore them to use English, the leader of the group responds, "But teacher, we're finished." How would you respond and why?

Multimedia-Based Lessons

Multimedia includes video, audio, books, magazines, websites, stories, photos, newspapers, and other realia.

Multimedia-Based Lesson: The Desk Set

Level: Intermediate +

Language Focus: New and familiar vocabulary

Skills Focus: Listening and speaking practice, critical reflection

Materials: DVD or VCD of *Dead Poet's Society*, DVD or VCD player and screen, handout with a few questions related to the scene

All students appreciate the opportunity to see and hear authentic English spoken by native speakers whenever possible. By planning lessons based on movie clips, you provide your students the added benefit of participating in activities with entertainment value. In the following plan, a clip from a popular movie is used to prompt students to reflect on education in their own culture. Visual materials work well in stimulating reflection and follow-up discussion.

Warm-Up Activity: Birthday presents

Invite your students to share the worst birthday present they have ever received with the class. Then, in groups of 4 or 6 have students create a bad birthday present to give to another group. You can reward the group which creates the worst birthday present.

Activity 1: Listening and cloze reading

Students watch a selected scene in which a boy attempts to cheer his friend after the latter has received a desk set for his birthday from his parents. It is the same item his parents gave him the previous year. He is disheartened, and his friend consoles him.

The teacher provides each student with a script of the scene. The script should contain several blanks. As the students watch the movie, they should listen carefully to fill in the blanks (cloze reading). The teacher may need to play the movie twice or read the complete script slowly in his/her own voice.

Activity 2: Dialogue practice

With a partner, students take turns reading the script trying to imitate the exact pronunciation of the boy and his friend. Students then switch roles and practice reading the dialogue a second time.

Activity 3: Role play

Students turn over their scripts and create a similar dialogue with their partner who has received a bad birthday gift. Students can use some of the same vocabulary or questions from the original script, but should attempt to make a new and creative scene of their own. Ample time should be given for students to practice and act out their dialogues. The teacher should circulate the role to ensure maximum participation. As the activity winds down, the teacher invites pairs to perform their role plays in front of the class. Following each role play, the teacher should call on students at random to ensure comprehension of the others' role plays.

Activity 4: Discussion

In groups of 4 to 6 students discuss ideal birthday gifts for: friends, teachers, parents, children, lovers, and siblings. Groups then explain their choices in front of the class.

Multimedia-Based Lesson 2: Friends

Level: Pre-intermediate +

Language Focusv: New and familiar vocabulary, adjectives

Skills Focus: Reading practice, reflecting on the values of friendship

Warm-Up Activity: Quick write

Students are given five minutes to compose a list of as many adjectives as they can think of that describe a true friend (e.g., kind, nice, honest). Elicit examples from class at random and write on the board. Check to be sure everyone understands the adjectives. (Alternatively, you could begin this lesson by asking students about the characters from the American TV sitcom, *Friends*, and write adjectives describing each character on the board.)

Chapter 4 Adapting and Revising Lesson Plans

Activity 1: Reading a story

When teaching a class of beginners, you may want to distribute copies of the stories to your students before reading it. Read the following story slowly and clearly, and, if possible, with a theatrical flair.

Friends

A story tells of two friends walking through the desert. During the journey they had an argument and one friend slapped the other in the face. The friend who was slapped felt hurt, but without saying anything, wrote in the sand: TODAY MY BEST FRIEND SLAPPED ME IN THE FACE. (Write this sentence on the board.)

They continued to walk until they found an oasis, a clear pool surrounded by palm trees. The friends decided to stop and take a bath. The one who had been slapped got stuck in quicksand and started drowning, but his friend grabbed his arm and pulled him to safety. After he had recovered from his near drowning, the friend wrote on a stone: TODAY MY BEST FRIEND SAVED MY LIFE. (Write this sentence on the board.) The friend who had slapped and then saved his best friend asked him, "After I hurt you, you wrote in the sand and now, you write on a stone. Why?"

The first friend replied, "When someone hurts us, we should write it down in sand where winds of forgiveness can erase it away. But, when someone does something good for us, we must engrave it in stone where no wind can ever erase it."

Activity 2: Vocabulary

In pairs, match the word on the left with the definition on the right.

1	Slap	A	To write something permanently in stone
2	Forgiveness	B	Sand in which you can sink down
3	Argument	C	To pardon another person
4	Engrave	D	To sink in water and die
5	Oasis	E	To strike someone with your open hand
6	Erase	F	Wet and green place in the desert
7	Quicksand	G	To fight with words
8	Drown	H	To cancel something

Activity 3: Comprehension Check

Student A: What does kind mean?

Teacher: Can someone define kind? What does it mean to be a kind friend?

Student B: It means to be very close to your friend.

Teacher: OK, anyone else?

Student C: It means friendly.

Activity 4: Homework

Write a story you remember about you and your best friend. Did you learn anything from this incident?

Reflection and Activity for Teachers

1. What do you like about the two multimedia-based lesson plans above?
2. Would you revise anything about his plan? Explain what and why.
3. If your students have never written a story in English before, how could you better prepare them for the homework in Activity 4?

Shenzhen Education Bureau and CTLC leaders and coordinators assignment meeting

Language Acquisition

Chapter 5

The goals for this chapter are:
- To better understand what is meant by fluency in a foreign language.
- To understand Krashen's *i + 1* theory and the natural approach.
- To create practical classroom applications of language acquisition theory.

Reflection:

In my first months teaching English in China, I would spend laborious hours creating a detailed lesson plan and acting it out in my mind. I would teach the same lesson to different classes, following the same routine each time. I believed that through repetition and practice I could create a perfect lesson that I could implement perfectly in each and every class I taught. Through practice, continual refinement, and repetition, I could become a perfect teacher. How naïve I was! Sometimes the same lesson plan was well received by one class and totally rejected by another. One class would praise my teaching style while another class would yawn in my face. What I had failed to realize was that teaching has very little to do with the teacher and a whole lot more to do with the individual classes and students—how and what they wanted to learn. The more I talked to my students, got to know their strengths and weaknesses, and developed my lessons to meet their needs and wants, the better my teaching became. It's like a restaurant where a chef spends endless hours perfecting only the dishes he or she wants to eat. The chef may be truly expert, but the restaurant will likely go out of business very soon. Compare that to a chef who cooks *for* her customers, displays concern for *their* preferences above her own, questions them about *their* likes and dislikes, *listens* to their criticisms, and adapts her cooking to meet the needs and wants of her clients. The key to professional language teaching is listening to your students and assessing their linguistic needs and wants. It's really that simple.

Fluency

What does it mean to be fluent in another language? I was born in the U.S. and have spoken English throughout my entire life. Most people would say I was "fluent" in English. However, if I were asked to speak before a conference on biomedical engineering or art history of the 16th century, you would quickly find limitations in my vocabulary, length and speed of speaking. After 12 years of Chinese language study, I can speak fairly quickly and at some length on basic topics like food, school, and travel. Ask me to discuss architecture, engineering, or even language acquisition in Chinese, and you'd think I'd never even been to China. Spanish is my most proficient second language, but I consciously avoid future tense, make frequent mistakes with reflexive verbs, and never can roll my *r*'s like a native Spanish speaker. Does fluency mean perfectly acquiring all aspects (vocabulary, syntax, speed, pronunciation, etc.) of the language? Or does fluency mean speaking a certain number of words per minute? Or does it mean thinking in the target language without first filtering through another language? Or does fluency mean speaking at a level appropriate to one's age and education?

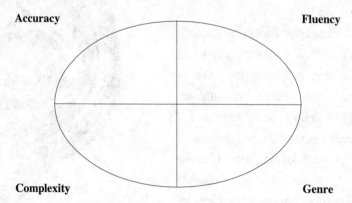

TEFL instructors typically define **fluency** as **the ability to speak at ample length and speed**. However, we realize that speaking quickly for a long time does mean you've acquired a language. **Accuracy** is defined as **the recognition and proper use of a language's syntax and vocabulary**. Typically, beginning second language learners fall into one of two categories: (1) those who speak a lot, speak relatively quickly, but make a lot of mistakes, and (2) those who display such great concern for using the correct word or sentence structure that they speak sl-o-o-o-o-w-ly and briefly, but make fewer mistakes. We should recognize that both **fluency** and **accuracy** are important to acquiring a language. However, these two components are often placed in direct conflict. If a teacher constantly instructs students to correct their vocabulary and syntax, their **accuracy** may improve, but they may also become so self-conscious of their mistakes that they begin to speak less and less. In contrast, if a teacher continually encourages her students to "Speak more!" or "Speak faster!", students' fluency may increase, but they're also going to make a lot more mistakes. To complicate matters, at the high-school or college-level, TEFL instructors will often complain when their second language learners write research papers or choose to debate on "unacademic" topics like the best vacation spot, their favorite sport, why dogs are better pets than cats, or generic platitudes like life needs adventure or success requires 100% effort. Although at this level, their writing and speech comes quickly, with relatively few grammar or vocabulary mistakes, and filling 10 minutes or 3 pages presents no problem, the ideas are fairly elementary, the sentence structures relatively short and simple, and the argumentative support nearly non-existent. In other words, their language lacks **complexity**. **Complexity** is defined as **the use of various syntactical structures to express deeper, audience-appropriate, and less black-and-white ideas**. I sometimes read a student's paper and think the ideas would be considered fairly complex for a 7th grade class, but lack the complexity expected for a university freshman. The final component of language acquisition is genre. I once helped edit research papers written by medical doctors in South Korea who wanted to publish in some of the top science journals in the world. Unfortunately, 70-90% of the top science journals are published only in English. These doctors could give top-notch 20 minute presentations at international conferences, explicate surgical procedures or various new biomedical engineering technologies that made my head spin. However, when stuck in elevator with a stranger, they barely knew how to introduce themselves or make small talk. **Genre** is defined as the **conventional linguistic expectations inherent to a certain profession, field of study, or group**. TEFL instructors have a certain way of talking; we use certain acronyms, words, and short-hand structures that differ dramatically from electrical engineers or art history majors. These linguistic conventions set us apart from others, help to delineate our field of study from other fields, and establish us a unique and distinctive community. There are numerous genres involved in language acquisition, and unfortunately, students at a very young will often develop a strong bias toward one particular **genre** when it comes to learning a second language. "Why do we have to speak? Speaking isn't on the national exam. I only want to learn the English required for the national exam," one of your students may likely complain at some point during the next year. "I'm not interested in reading this story; I want to be an engineer, not a literature professor!" another student may declare. Or, "I don't like history; I want to talk about sports." What these students are really pointing out is that different **genres** require different language.

Hopefully, by now you realize just how complicated language acquisition or being "fluent" in a language really is. **Fluency**, **accuracy**, **complexity**, and **genre** are four equal components of language acquisition. While advanced language learners can manage and balance the interactions between the four components, intermediate and low-level language learners tend to compartmentalize the four components.

So how does this affect how we teach fluency in English to our Chinese students? Well, obviously the more your students write and speak, the better their writing and speaking will be. But...

1. Fluency without accuracy, complexity, or generic conventions matched to your audience's expectations is solipsistic (unless you're James Joyce and even he...).
2. EFL students aren't inherently aware of English syntax and expected generic conventions.
3. EFL students will often write to a level of complexity where their accuracy and fluency is not challenged.
4. Writing a poem, a lab report, a historical essay, and an economic research paper require different strategies and different generic structures.
5. If you write/speak, correct, write/speak, correct, and write/speak correct, your fluency and love for learning English will suffer.

Surely, you ask, there must be a more systematic approach to acquire a second language? Luckily, there is...

Stephen Krashen and the Natural Approach

Stephen Krashen was my former undergraduate professor at University of Southern California. I didn't understand at the time why his classes were filled to capacity, but today I'm very fortunate to have attended his lectures. His research and theories into language acquisition are tremendously influential for all TEFL instructors. Plus, they're pretty easy to understand, and more, importantly to apply in reality.

According to Krashen's theories, language acquisition happens best when:

- Input is provided at the *i + 1* level.
- The affective filter is lowered.
- The monitor is not made too strong by an overemphasis on accuracy.
- The natural order of acquisition is respected.

In the *i + 1* schema, *i* means **interlanguage**, the point on the continuum between L1 and L2 that the learner currently occupies. *+1* means that the input should be just a little more complex or challenging than the learner can easily comprehend.

Chapter 5 Language Acquisition

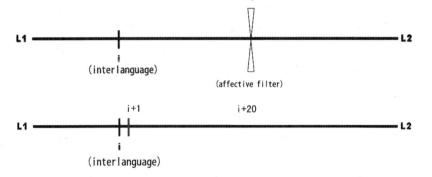

Let's use skiing as an example. I only started skiing last year; I've been skiing a total of seven times in my life. Last weekend, my uncle, who skis 4—5 times a week during the winter, has skied for over 50 years, and has conquered nearly every trail from Utah to Vermont, invited me skiing. While he could have led me down the scariest, triple black diamond run in the park and showed off his expertise while I slid my way down the mountain, he obviously did not do this. Why not? Because this would have been + 100 steps beyond my starting input level. Instead, he led me to the beginner's slope and assessed my skills. When he saw that I could ski down the beginner slope without falling (which to me, meant skiing), we went back to the top of the beginner slope and he showed me how to hold my poles in front of me rather than dangling to the sides. That was it. One step. I practiced skiing the beginning slope several times, just concentrating on holding my poles in the correct position. When my uncle saw that I had mastered that lesson, he taught me how to bend my knees properly. That was it. Second step. And, thus, by the weekend's end, while I wasn't flying down the most difficult runs in the park, I had noticeably improved in several small steps from my starting point. Language acquisition occurs in much the same way: one small step at a time.

New instructors fail to appreciate the importance of *i* +*1*. They fail to assess their students' starting input level, thus resulting in one of two common problems. (1) Creating lesson plans that are over the heads of the students, which leads to raised negative affected filters, boredom, behavior problems, negative views of the teacher and English in general, and (2) creating lesson plans that are below or on par with what students already know, which leads to boredom, behavior problems, negative views of the teacher and English. You want to teach your students something new, not repeat or dumb down something they've already learned. However, you don't want to teach your students something that they are not ready to learn—something that will only confuse or frustrate them. You want to challenge them step by step without losing them along the way.

This is what is meant by *i* + *1*, and why most experienced teachers will spend some time during the first few meetings of a class to informally and/or formally assess students' starting L2 input levels. Simple questions like, "What have you been studying in your other English class?" "What did you study last year?" or "Can you show me the chapters in the textbook that you've already covered?" can go a long way in helping you assess your students' *i* level.

When a student is nervous or frightened in the language class, a **filter** goes up that prevents the input from getting through. The teacher can lower the **affective filter** by making the classroom a safe, comfortable environment in which the student feels that she can take risks in using the L2. When the input from the lesson is far beyond $i + 1$, an **affective filter** immediately goes up that discourages even the most diligent of students from acquiring the lesson.

The **monitor** is the part of the brain that checks language output for accuracy. As we have already seen, an overly strong monitor interferes with fluency because the learner is overly concerned about getting the grammar, pronunciation, vocabulary correct. Constant correct or over-focusing on accuracy by the teacher strengthens the **monitor**, and as a result, inhibits fluency.

Reflection and Activity for Teachers

1. Since students are likely to be at very different levels of "i" within the same class, what does that mean for the teacher and the planning of classroom activities?
2. What steps can you take as a teacher to lower your students' affective filter?
3. What steps can you take as a teacher to lower your students' monitor?

Natural Order of Acquisition

Research shows that many elements of English syntax are acquired in a certain order regardless of when they are taught. For example, the plural and possessive "s" endings are usually acquired before the 3rd person singular "s." Effective teachers can speed up the process of language acquisition but not change the order in which certain linguistic elements are acquired.

Krashen divides the natural order of acquisition into 4 stages: Pre-Production, Early Production, Speech Emergence, and Intermediate Fluency.

Pre-Production

Just because your students aren't speaking doesn't mean they aren't acquiring language. Most babies don't say their first word until 9 - 12 months of age. And their first words are always garbled. Yet, this whole time babies are listening, absorbing language, processing it through their developing minds. Although you won't be teaching babies, many of your Chinese students are likely to be in the pre-production stage of language acquisition. Their comprehension skills are minimal and they can barely speak more than a few words. This is not because they are mentally deficient or bad students, but because the language is so new to them and they've had very few opportunities to practice it. While these learners may be unable to produce language, they can

- Point

- Draw
- Chant/sing
- Respond with action (Simon Says)
- Listen and repeat
- Act out to show they understand

With such learners, teachers should:

- Use visual aids and **realia** (posters, collages, clay, crayons, etc.)
- Modify speech (speak louder, slower, and more clearly)
- Use activities with physical responses
- Focus on building vocabulary

Early Production

At this stage of language acquisition, students can understand more and can produce one or two word answers. Students can:

- Name
- Label
- Group
- List
- Categorize
- Count
- Sort
- Answer "yes" or "no"
- Answer with a word or two

With such learners, teachers should:

- Ask yes/no questions
- Accept one word answers
- Use fill-in-the-blank exercises
- Build slowly to expand students' answers
- Expect mistakes that show developing acquisition

Speech Emergence

At this next stage, students can produce phrases and complete sentences. Students can:

- Retell
- Define
- Explain

- Compare/contrast
- Summarize/paraphrase
- Describe
- Role-play

With such learners, teachers should:

- Provide input through reading and listening.
- Use games and problem-solving activities.
- Introduce writing exercises.
- Use language familiar to students.
- Expect some basic errors in speech and writing.

Intermediate Fluency

Now, students can create longer passages of language, both written and verbal. Students can:

- Analyze
- Create
- Defend
- Debate
- Predict

- Evaluate
- Justify
- Support
- Examine
- Hypothesize

With such learners, teachers should:
- Use activities that require higher level thinking skills.
- Expect some errors, especially in writing, although communication will be fairly clear.

Reflection and Activity for Teachers

1. Choose two of the verbs under the "Students can" listing for each of the four stages. Think of two activities for each stage that would allow students to do the recommended action in their L2. Share your activities with your group and then with the rest of the class.
2. What does it mean to be fluent in a second language (L2)? What level of English fluency do you anticipate your students to have?
3. What do we mean by $i + 1$? Describe to your group $i + 1$, a natural approach to children first learning a new language.

Multiple Intelligences

Chapter 6

The goals for this chapter are:
- To better understand what is meant by multiple intelligences.
- To imagine numerous ways of attacking a single language objective.
- To practice numerous ways of attacking a specific skills focus.

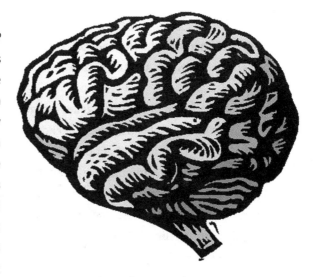

What does it mean to be intelligent? Being a recent college graduate, this question passed across my thoughts more than once in relation to my new job as a TEFL teacher. Teaching was hard and my Chinese students seemed to learn differently from me. Wait a second! Some things come natural and other things don't... well, that's a lot like first and second languages. Some people can learn a new language faster than others. Does this make them more intelligent or just naturally gifted? In contrast, some people can learn a musical instrument quickly. Is this intelligence or a natural gift? Is being physically gifted to run 100m in under 10 seconds intelligence?

Multiple Intelligences

Teachers have long recognized that students have different strengths and weaknesses. In the field of language learning, some of these differences have been attributed to learning styles. For instance some students are better visual learners than aural learners. Psychologist Howard Gardner's theory of multiple intelligences promotes the diversity of approaches by which students learn a new language. Although Gardner describes seven intelligences, recent researchers suggest many more intelligences. By understanding multiple intelligences we can understand how our TEFL students learn and acquire a second language most effectively.

Note: Multiple intelligences are essential to teaching young language learners!!!

Warm-up Activity for Teachers

Find someone in the class who can do the following. They must perform the task, not just say they can do it.

1. Whistle the chorus to any Michael Jackson song.
2. Stand on one foot with eyes closed and arms raised for ten seconds.
3. Recite at least four lines from any poem.
4. Draw a diagram to show how a car engine works.
5. Share a detailed dream they have had in the past two weeks.
6. Complete this sequence: 8, 66, 4358, ...
7. Name five flowering plants common in their hometown.
8. Honestly claim to be relaxed and comfortable relating to other people during this exercise.

■ **Verbal/Linguistic Intelligence**: Likes to write papers and letters. Learns through reading. Needs to see words written before remembering them. Enjoys stories, word play, reading and writing.

■ **Logical/Mathematical Intelligence**: Is good with numbers and logic. Learns through solving puzzles, problems. Likes to know expectations in terms of rules, routines, and assignments. Likes to read about new developments in science.

■ **Musical/Rhythmic Intelligence**: Likes to sing, play a musical instrument and listen to music. Learns the sounds and rhythms of language through songs, chants. May have an easy time mastering stress and intonation.

■ **Body/Kinesthetic Intelligence**: Learns through movement, dance, and physical manipulation. Needs to connect language to movements, gestures, pointing out, matching pictures to words physically, acting out scenes, dialogues, etc.

■ **Visual/Spatial Intelligence**: Likes to take photographs, draw pictures. Has a good spatial

sense, can find way around easily. Learns through visual aids, illustrations, charts, graphs.
- **Interpersonal Intelligence**: Prefers doing things with other people to being alone. Solves problems by discussing with friends. Learns through interaction with others, discussions, group work.
- **Intrapersonal Intelligence**: Likes to reflect, meditate, keep a journal. Prefers to use own methods in studying/mastering new materials. Learns through reflection, independent work, using own learning strategies.

A Multiple Intelligences Inventory for Adults

Take the multiple intelligences inventory below; then share your results with the class. Place an "x" next to those statements that apply to you. Use these intelligence categories to help you understand your strongest types of intelligence as well as your strengths and weaknesses.

Verbal/Linguistic Intelligence
1. _____ Books are very important to me.
2. _____ I can hear words in my head before I read, speak, or write them down.
3. _____ I get more out of listening to the radio or a spoken-word podcast than I do from television or films.
4. _____ I enjoy words games like Scrabble, Boggle, Anagrams, or crossword puzzles.
5. _____ I enjoy entertaining myself or others with tongue twisters, nonsense rhymes, or puns.
6. _____ Other people sometimes have to stop and ask me to explain the meaning of the words I use in my writing and speaking.
7. _____ English, social studies, and history were for me in school than math or science.
8. _____ When I drive down a freeway, I pay more attention to the words written on signs than to the scenery.
9. _____ My conversation includes frequent references to things that I've read or heard.
10. _____ I've written something recently that I was particularly proud of or that earned me recognition from others.
SCORE:_____

Body/Kinesthetic Intelligence
1. _____ I engage in at least one sport or physical activity on a regular basis.
2. _____ I find it difficult to sit still for long periods of time.
3. _____ I like working at manual activities such as sewing, weaving, carving, carpentry, or model building.
4. _____ My best ideas often come to me when I'm out for a long walk or when I'm engaged in some other kind of physical activity.
5. _____ I like to spend my free time outdoors.

6. _____ I frequently use hand gestures or other forms of body language when conversing with someone.
7. _____ I need to touch things in order to learn more about them.
8. _____ I enjoy daredevil amusement rides or similar thrilling physical experiences.
9. _____ I would describe myself as well-coordinated.
10. _____ I need to practice a new skill rather than simply reading about it or seeing a video that describes it.

SCORE:_____

Logical/Mathematical Intelligence

1. _____ I can easily compute numbers in my head.
2. _____ Math and/or science were among my favorite subject(s) in school.
3. _____ I enjoy playing games or solving brainteasers that require logical thinking.
4. _____ I like to set up little "what if" experiments (i.e., "What if I double the amount of water I give my houseplant each week?"
5. _____ My mind searches for patterns, regularities, or logical sequences in things.
6. _____ I'm interested in new developments in science.
7. _____ I believe that almost everything has a rational explanation.
8. _____ I sometimes think in clear abstract, wordless, imageless concepts.
9. _____ I like finding logical flaws in things that people say and do.
10. _____ I feel more comfortable when something has been measured, categorized, analyzed, or quantified in some way.

SCORE:_____

Intrapersonal Intelligence

1. _____ I regularly spend time alone meditating, reflecting, or thinking about life questions.
2. _____ I have attended counseling sessions or personal growth seminars to learn about myself.
3. _____ I am able to respond to setbacks with resilience.
4. _____ I have a special hobby or interest that I keep pretty much to myself.
5. _____ I have some important goals for my life that I think about on a regular basis.
6. _____ I have a realistic view of my strengths and weaknesses (borne out by feedback from other sources).
7. _____ I would prefer to spend a weekend alone in a cabin in the woods rather than at a fancy resort with lots of people around.
8. _____ I consider myself to be strong willed or independent minded.
9. _____ I keep a personal diary or journal to record the events of my inner life.
10. _____ I am self-employed or have at least seriously thought about starting my own business.

SCORE:_____

Chapter 6 Multiple Intelligences

Musical/Rhythmic Intelligence
1. _____ I have a pleasant singing voice.
2. _____ I can tell when a musical note is off-key.
3. _____ I frequently listen to music on the radio, CD, internet, or iPod.
4. _____ I play a musical instrument.
5. _____ My life would be poorer if there were no music in it.
6. _____ I sometimes catch myself walking around with a jingle or other tune running through my mind.
7. _____ I can easily keep time to a piece of music with a simple percussion instrument.
8. _____ I know the tunes to many different songs or music pieces.
9. _____ If I hear a musical selection once or twice, I am able to sing it back fairly accurately.
10. _____ I often make tapping sounds or sing little melodies while working, studying, or learning something new.

SCORE: _____

Visual/Spatial Intelligence
1. _____ I often see clear visual images when I close my eyes.
2. _____ I'm sensitive to color.
3. _____ I frequently use a camera or camcorder to record what I see around me.
4. _____ I enjoy doing jigsaw puzzles, mazes, and other visual puzzles.
5. _____ I have vivid dreams at night.
6. _____ I can generally find my way around unfamiliar territory.
7. _____ I like to draw or doodle.
8. _____ In school, geometry was easier for me than algebra.
9. _____ I can imagine how something might appear if it were looked down upon from directly above in a bird's-eye view.
10. _____ I prefer looking at reading material that is heavily illustrated.

SCORE: _____

Interpersonal Intelligence
1. _____ I'm the sort of person that people often come to for advice.
2. _____ I prefer group sports like volleyball or softball to solo sports such as swimming or biking.
3. _____ When I have a problem, I'm more likely to seek out another person for help than attempt to work it out on my own.
4. _____ I have at least three close friends.
5. _____ I favor social pastimes such as Monopoly or poker over individual recreations such as video games and solitaire.
6. _____ I enjoy the challenge of teaching other people what I know how to do.
7. _____ I feel comfortable in the midst of a crowd.

8. _____ I consider myself a leader (or others have called me that).
9. _____ I like to get involved in social activities connected with my work, church, or community.
10. _____ I would rather spend my evenings at a lively party than stay at home alone.
SCORE:_____

> **Reflection and Activity for Teachers**
>
> 1. Think of three activities you have used or experienced in a language class. What intelligence did those activities use?
> 2. Imagine you are teaching a primary school class about days of the week. Think of one activity for each multiple intelligence that you could use in class.

CTLC teachers´ Contract Signing Ceremony

Methodology

Chapter 7

The goals for this chapter are:
- To better understand the benefits and detriments of a grammar translation method (GTM).
- To better understand the benefits and detriments of a communicate language teaching (CLT) method.
- To discuss methods of teaching with knowledge, understanding, and wisdom.

The Big Divide:

Years after the Latin language was pronounced "dead," its syntax is still being taught in language classes. It is hoped that through the study of the grammar of a second language (L2), students would become familiar with the grammar of their first language (L1). In addition, this grammatical familiarity would help them speak and write better in both languages (Larsen-Freeman, 2000). All living languages (and even a few dead ones) possess grammar. TEFL teachers can all agree that grammar is an important part of L2 acquisition. But how important is grammar to learning a language? Well, there's a big divide among TEFL teachers in response to that question.

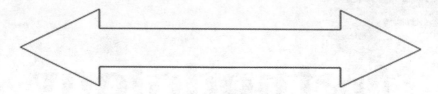

Teaching

- Teacher directs / students receive. Teacher-centered approach.
- Grammar and vocabulary are taught explicitly.
- Language of instruction is the L1.
- No individualization, no alternatives, no questioning of the teacher's authority.
- Reward and punishment based on conformity to teacher's lesson.
- Rote memorization of grammar and vocabulary.
- Frequent drills, memorization of famous passages, and translation of passages from classic texts.
- No or little speaking /listening practice.
- Dictation exercises.

- Teacher facilitates or moderates/ students direct. Student-centered approach.
- Grammar and vocabulary are taught implicitly.
- Language of instruction is usually the L2.
- Topics are personally meaningful to students; learning approached as personal discovery; students become teachers.
- Multiple answers exit.
- Focus is on fluency and production, less on accuracy.
- Emphasis on using authentic material.
- Students are challenged to speak as much as possible.
- Teachers often elicit language items from students.

Grammar Translation Method

Manysecond language learners, and especially those of older generations, grew up believing that an L2 can only taught through austere drills and repetition. Of course, there was little scientific evidence to support this widespread pedagogical theory, but that's just how things were. Teachers taught a language in the exact same way that they were taught when they were children. The **grammar translation method** (**GTM**)—at least until the 1970s—was the world's most popular method for TEFL instruction. In China, GTM remains the primary method of English instruction although its popularity may be on the wane. GTM instruction typically prizes **accuracy** in a language above **fluency**.

One of the reasons GTM remains the preferred method of TEFL instruction in China is that GTM has proven itself as a reliable method for preparing students for the state English exams. The national exam, which consist mainly of grammar and vocabulary exercises, lacks a speaking component. It is common for students who learn this way to be able to recite long passages of

Chapter 7 Methodology

English literature by heart; however, they struggle to communicate verbally in everyday, authentic contexts. In the United States there has been a revival of GTM in the recent past.

It's important to avoid black-and-white arguments concerning language teaching methodology. While I may appear critical of GTM, I cannot deny its effectiveness and widespread popularity, especially in the teaching of grammar, vocabulary, and standardized test preparation. However, in my mind, overreliance on GTM can negatively affect students' fluency and intrinsic motivation to learn English. The adverse results of a GTM-centered approach are omnipresent in both American and Chinese language classrooms. They include an emphasis on reception (reading and listening) and a de-emphasis on production (speaking and writing), an accentuation of accuracy at the expense of fluency, a dependence on course books rather than authentic conversation, a test-based instruction orientation rather than students' self-selected research and critical discussion, teacher-centered rather than student-centered learning (i.e., students come to rely on the teacher for approval, reward, or punishment; as a result, little independent learning takes place when the teacher is not present), compartmentalization of language results in high monitor and gaps in language abilities. GTM is not inherently evil; in fact, it can be quite effective in certain settings and for certain lesson plans. It's important to realize that the goal of any good TEFL teacher is to help students meet their needs. For many Chinese students, the goal of learning English is to get a high test score on the national exam, to improve their grammar and vocabulary rather than become near-native speakers of a language that is not used—and will never be used—in their daily lives.

Below is an example of a GTM-type activity. The teacher would explain the grammar rules and then instruct the students to fill-in-the-blank in accordance with the rules. The teacher would then collect the test, correct all errors, and give students a grade which they believe reflects their acquisition of the target language.

Past Tense Practice

1. Every day I walk. Yesterday I _____
2. Every day I cook. Yesterday I _____
3. Every day I add.   Yesterday I _____
4. Every day I subtract. Yesterday I _____
5. Every day I drive. Yesterday I _____

Six Bad Reasons for Teaching via GTM

1. It's easy for teachers to show off their expertise. Grammar teachers are prone to labeland correct every grammatical mistake whereas native speakers only correct mistakes that interfere with meaning.
2. It's tidy. There's only one correct answer. Teaching and testing grammar is much easier than teaching and testinglinguistic fluency.
3. Grammar serves as a security blanket; it's understandable and comfortable. It allows us

to think we have control over language.
4. That's the way I was taught in school. It made me who I am.
5. Grammar can be taught as an entire system.
6. Power. It allows the teacher to stand as the gatekeeper of correct English usage. Students must adapt their language to match that of the teacher.

Two Good Reasons for Teaching via GTM

1. It's historically proven to work for large numbers of Chinese students attempting to pass the English national exam.
2. One's individual language must be acceptable and comprehensible to the norms or expectations of the community. Just as few American males wear skirts in public without fear of public censure, few native English speakers would accept "you is" or "she go" as normal, correct English. Notice: this is not to say that wearing a skirt would be less comfortable or practical or that "you is" or "she go" is wrong (in fact, both are correct when directly translated into Chinese). However, language is communal and there are norms and expectations that every discourse community has for speaking and writing. "Correct" grammar is one normal expectation that every linguistic community seems to prefer.

Communicative Language Teaching

At the opposite end of the TEFL methodological spectrum, we can find Communicative Language Teaching (**CLT**). **CLT** is a method which has grown in popularity since the 1970s. CLT is centered on helping students not merely to know the language, but to apply what they know in communicative contexts. CLT approaches are known as student-centered instruction because, in contrast to GTM, it is the students who are at the center of the learning process. CLT is founded on a learning-by-doing approach.

The communicative approach to classroom teaching goes a long way toward facilitating communicative competence when compared to earlier methods which targeted the same objective. Teaching students how to use the language is considered to be at least as important as learning the language itself. Brown (1994) aptly describes the march toward CLT, which might be considered the CLT teacher's missions statement:

> Beyond grammatical discourse elements in communication, we are probing the nature of social, cultural, and pragmatic features of language. We are exploring pedagogical means for "real-life" communication in the classroom. We are trying to get our learners to develop linguistic fluency, not just the accuracy that has so consumed our historical journey. We are equipping our students with the tools for generating unrehearsed language performance "out there" when they leave the womb of our classrooms. We are concerned with how to

facilitate lifelong language learning among our students, not just with the immediate classroom task. We are looking at learners as partners in a cooperative venture. And our classroom practices seek to draw on whatever intrinsically sparks learners to reach their fullest potential.

Below is a sample lesson plan outlining one of my most popular communicative games. See how this game approaches grammar through a more communicative classroom approach. Compare this sample activity to the GTM sample activity above. Which activity requires more speaking from the students? Which activity will be most effective for your students' needs and aims?

Alibi Game

- Approach: Communicative Language Teaching
- Level: low-intermediate to advanced, any age
- Language Objective: Speaking + accuracy + past tense verbs + increasing fluency
- Skills Focus: Speaking complete sentences + asking follow-up questions + listening for accuracy
- Estimated Time: 30-50 minutes

Where were you last night between 7 and 11 pm?
Who were you with?
How did you get there?
When did you arrive?
When did you leave?
What did you see/buy/do?
Why did you go there?
Where did you go next?
What were you wearing?
Who saw you?

1. Warm-up activity (3—5 min.): Teacher asks students about their weekend or past night activities (e.g., What did you do last night? Who were you with? When did you leave?). Students will typically give short, simple answers and fail to ask questions of their own to the teacher.

2. Introduction of today's language objective/skills focus, teacher models correct use (3~5 min.): A good conversation involves two people asking questions, showing interest in listening to their partners, and asking follow-up questions. Try again with one student in class.

3. Instructions: Last night someone killed the teacher between 6 and 11pm. The police suspect the murderer was someone in the class due to a note found on the body criticizing TEFL conversation class. Students must work in pairs (Partner A and B) to create a detailed alibi. After 10 minutes, the police (another pair) will come to question both partners. Both partners (A and B) must have the same story and correctly use the past tense.

4. Activity #1: Pair work (10 min.) Partners compose their alibis. For low-level classes, teacher can model the target language on the board (e.g., Last night, I went to ____. I ate ____.) For higher level classes no modeling is required and teacher should encourage greater detail in students' alibis.
5. Activity #2: Partner A questions Partner C, Partner B questions Partner D (5 min.). Questions and answers should be given in complete sentences. Failure to correctly use the past tense more than three times will result in the student being sent to "jail."
6. Activity #3: Partner C questions Partner A, Partner D questions Partner A (5 min.).
7. Activity #4: Partner A questions Partner D, Partner B questions Partner C (5 min.). Remember the alibis should be identical. Police should note the similarities and differences between the two alibis.
8. Activity #5: Each student files a written or oral report of the differences and similarities between the two alibis, using complete sentences and past tense (20~25 min.).
9. Students summarize/review the lesson (2~3 min.).

Reflection and Activity for Teachers

1. What are some of the characteristic differences between the Grammar Translation and Communicative Language Teaching methods? Do you think both methods are equally effective in serving their respective aims?
2. Both methods arose to meet very different language goals. Do you think you will use both of the methods in your teaching in China? If so, what language learning objectives do you hope to achieve by using these methods? Explain.
3. How do you think your students in China will respond to the two methods?
4. The majority of your Chinese students will be accustomed to GTM approaches. How can Chinese students get accustomed to learning English through CLT?

Total Physical Response (TPR)

The founder of the Total Physical Response (TPR), James Asher (1977) observed that children, in acquiring their first language, seem to do a lot of listening before they speak, and their listening is accompanied by physical responses (reaching, grabbing, moving, looking, and so on). TPR methods seek to create a stress-free classroom environment, one similar to the environment most children experience in learning their native language.

In the TPR-based classroom, the teacher is seen as a director and the students as actors. The teacher orchestrates the performance carried out by the students with a series of commands: open the window, close the door, sit down, stand up, pick up the book, and give it to John. In addition to imperatives, interrogatives are also often used: Where is the book? Who is John? Humor is easily introduced and the method lends itself to promoting a playful learning environment. Today TPR is often viewed more as a technique and is especially successful in teaching children.

In the communicative classroom, TPR can be used as a way of accommodating the silent period and allowing students to demonstrate understanding before they are ready to produce new vocabulary and structures. It provides a safe environment where learners can gradually accustom themselves to communicating in the target language.

Sample TPR Activities

Body Parts

1. Review the body parts, using a visual if possible.
2. Then play Simon Says. Have students stand beside their desks and respond to your commands when you say, "Simon says put your hand on your head." Tell them not to do the action if you don't say, "Simon says."
3. Play for a while, using most of the parts of the body you've reviewed.
4. If you have some students who can give the commands, have them rotate giving the commands.

TPR Listening

1. Choose a story with new vocabulary that can be drawn easily—animals, for example, or food. Introduce the vocabulary.
2. Have students draw pictures of the items on pieces of paper. If there are eight vocabulary words, one partner should draw four pictures and the other partner the other four pictures.
3. Read the story. When students hear the words that they have pictures for, they hold up their pictures.
4. Glance around the room to verify that each pair is holding up a picture. This focuses the students' attention on the story, as they are listening for their words to occur. If the story is short, read it two or three times with responses.

Prepositions of Place

1. Use objects students have on their desks. Start by demonstrating with one of your better students.
2. Say, "Put the pencil on the book." Prompt the students to place a pencil on a book. Say, "Put the pencil under the book."
3. Repeat several times with other objects and prepositions.
4. Write "Put the pencil" on the board.
5. Have students repeat together.
6. Prompt a good student to tell you, "Put the pencil on the book." (You can add "please.")
7. Tell students to practice with their partner telling each other to put the pencil on, in, beside, under, etc. other things on their desk.

Storytelling

TPR storytelling is a technique that can be used with more advanced language. Take some vocabulary from a story and teach students physical gestures that go with the vocabulary. The gestures can be symbolic or representational. For example, for a verb such as "walk" or "run," students can make a walking gesture with their first and second fingers. For "grandmother," they can hold out one hand like they are holding a cane to walk with, and so on. Practice several times by saying the words and having students perform the gestures. Follow up with other activities: have students act out the story in small groups, give students a fill-in-the-blank of the story with the vocabulary words left out. For more advanced students, have them create their own stories with the vocabulary and act out their own stories for the class.

Reflection and Activity for Teachers

1. Do you agree with Asher that foreign language instruction should be modeled on native language acquired? What are some of the characteristics of his method that are similar to the way children learn their L1?
2. How can TPR lower anxiety among students?
3. How would you use TPR in your teaching? Together with a partner, come up with a brief TPR activity aimed at teaching Days of the Week.

Director of the Culture and Education Department of National Foreign Expert Bureau Xia Bin gave a lecture to CTLC foreign teachers at Peking University summer training (CTLC Director William O'Donnell and Vice-Dean of PKU School of Foreign Languages Liu Shusen are in the back) 国家外专局文教司司长夏彬在北大对 CTLC 外教演讲

Nine Principles of TEFL

Chapter 8

The goals for this chapter are:
- To be able to objectively assess and evaluate YOUR OWN teaching and lesson plans.
- To recognize and implement the nine principles of TEFL in your lesson plans.

Nine Principles of TEFL

The following nine principles of TEFL represent a foundation upon which to build and implement effective lesson plans. These principles are especially relevant to teaching large classes, such as those you will encounter in your work in China.

PRINCIPLE 1: Personalization

Personalization means providing as many opportunities as possible for students to express their personal experiences, feelings, attitudes, likes/dislikes, and opinions. Teaching is a personal art. Don't hesitate to get to know your students and talk to them as people. It is important that your students feel that you view them individually and not just names on an attendance roster. Although this may seem a challenging proposition in a large class, there are a number of techniques which help students feel that their thoughts and feelings count. Research shows that students' assimilation of new material (such as a challenging foreign language) through their own personal opinions, hobbies, and interests results in a more effective learning process and aids memory.

From the very first day of your teaching, you'll want to get to know your students, their personalities, and their interests. I often ask students to write a letter of introduction on the first day. For lower-level classes, you may need to model the format of the letter and type of information you want included. Another option is to pass out notecards and ask students to write: (1) their name, (2) three topics they are interested in discussing, (3) two difficulties with English they would like to study more, (4) one topic they don't want to discuss. After collecting and reading these notecards, the teacher should have a better understanding of her students' likes and dislikes and certain topics for future classes. Here are some examples of activities that make effective use of personalization:

After reading about a controversial issue, I write a "Letter to the Editor" or a letter to another classmate about MY response to the reading!

Once a semester, I give a mini-presentation to the whole class about ME, MY personal hopes, MY dreams and MY career interests!

Yesterday, I talked about a person I admire: MY father.

I made a poster and researched about a country that I want to visit.

Personalizing Questions

The questions we pose to our students should also be personalized. We can use more effective language practice and sustain interest among our students by asking questions which are personally meaningful to them.

So, instead of asking, "Is English a difficult language to learn?" we can render the question more personally meaningful by asking, "What do you find most difficult about learning English?" We should emphasize the word *you* in order to elicit the students' personal feelings and opinions. "What do *you* think?" "What's *your* opinion about such and such?" "How do *you* feel about ...?"

> **Reflection and Activity for Teachers**
> 1. Getting personal. Together with a partner, try to imagine at least three personalized questions for the topics of music and Chinese customs. How might you build a communicative activity around these two topics?
> 2. Letter. With a different partner, design an activity in which students write a letter to someone about something of interest to them. They could write to an actor, sports figure, or someone they know. How would you devise a topic for the letters? Would you involve your class in deciding topics?

PRINCIPLE 2: Pace Your Activities

Classroom activities should proceed at a suitable tempo and momentum. Running students through an activity too fast or letting activities drag on too long can ruin the learning process. Some general rules of thumb to follow as new teachers growing accustomed to the pace of classroom teaching are:

- Drills should generally proceed briskly while discussions should move at a more leisurely pace.
- Students likely need more time than you think to perform the activity.
- Provide plenty of modeling and repetition—just because you're bored doesn't mean the students are.
- Watch for signs that you're moving too quickly or too slowly—if students are bored, behavior problems result.
- Watch for signs that the activity is winding down. Prepare to start the next activity.
- Don't be beholden to your own instructions or lesson plan.

Teaching is more like jazz than classical music. Through greater preparation and experience, teachers learn to recognize the flow of the lesson and begin to pace activities accordingly. A common trick is to provide time limits for instructions but to adapt the actual time in accordance with students' abilities and performance. For example, I might say, "You have 10 minutes to complete this task." In reality, however, I give only a cursory glance to my watch and announce that time has expired not when 10 minutes have passed but in accordance with the pace of the classroom, i.e., whether or not the students have acquired the targeted language or skill.

PRINCIPLE 3: Variety

Variety is the spice of life. The process of acquiring a language differs from learning other subjects, such as math or history. While studying a foreign language, students learn a foreign culture and test hypotheses about grammar and vocabulary both in real-life and simulated situations.

It follows that we should expose our students to a vast array of activities. We should remember not only to vary the activities we choose for our lessons but to vary our classroom and approaches as well. Most students cannot concentrate on a single activity for more than a limited length of time, no matter how interesting the subject. After a while, the mind naturally starts to wander. In large classes, such a lack of attention can prove disastrous. This does not mean that we cannot pursue the same subject matter or topic for an entire class period; it just means that we must vary the way in which we carry out the lesson. The principle of variety is essential in classroom management, as it helps activate quiet students while ensuring classroom control.To reach all learning styles and to prevent boredom, include a variety of topics, activities, techniques, and approaches. Here are some ways of introducing variety into your classroom:

- Alternate brisk, high-energy activities with slower, thoughtful activities.
- Follow a teacher-fronted activity with one involving pairs or small groups.
- Follow individual silent reading with verbal pair work based on the reading.
- If they have been working on something very challenging, give them something lighter.
- Repeat favorite games/activities at periodic intervals.

PRINCIPLE 4: Interesting Topics

When students find the lesson plan uninteresting, they are more likely to display disruptive behavior. Interesting lesson plans are of inherent value to the students and will help keep the students focused and engaged in the lesson. There are three features of topics that work particularly well with ESOL students. When planning our lessons, we can check to see if the topics we have chosen include at least one of the following features:

- Draw on students' personal experience, or
- Ask students to reflect on their own culture and attitudes, or
- Narrow the topic to make it more concrete and easier to discuss

Instead of instructing your students to discuss a general topic (e. g., culture, sports, entertainment), take time to create more interesting, concrete, authentic, and valuable questions for discussion. For example, "What are some cultural differences between living in Shenzhen and living in Hong Kong?" "Which soccer player is your favorite and why?" "How has the influx of American movies affected Chinese cinema?" The more thought and interest you put into your lesson plans, the more thought and interest your students will bring to their classwork.

> **Reflection and Activity for Teachers**
> 1. Choose three of the general topics from the list below and make them more interesting for a discussion activity. Try to make them meaningful for the age group and skill level you will be teaching in China.
>   Relationships   School is hard   Good manners   Famous people   Holidays
>   Language learning   Animals   Popular music   Fashion   Friends
> 2. How would you vary multiple activities centered upon one of your revised topics to create interest for all students in a large class?

PRINCIPLE 5: Collaboration

Cooperative learning or **collaborative learning** enables students to participate more, learn how to compromise, negotiate meaning, and become better risk-takers and more efficient self-monitors. In a large class where cooperation works better than competition, collaboration is a must (Hess, 2004). I like to say that there are 60 (or whatever the exact number of students in your class) teachers in my classroom and we all need to listen to and help each other to improve our English communication skills. Some classroom strategies that help students collaborate include:

> - group work in which students complete a task together,
> - pair work in which students share ideas or interview each other,
> - peer review in which students evaluate and comment on each other's written work,
> - brainstorming in which students contribute ideas on a single topic,
> - collaborative writing.

As teachers, especially in large classes, we simply cannot be everywhere to service the immediate needs of all students. Rather, we should encourage students to develop the habit of depending on one another as linguistic resources. In China, students are exposed mainly to teacher-centered styles of learning. Many will not be familiar with communicative, student-centered approaches aimed at eliciting personal opinions. Moreover, oral communication in pairs or groups may have actively discouraged in their prior English classes. As group discussion and authentic conversation are essential to students' acquisition of English, it is imperative that we establish routines to accustom our students to working in groups and speaking out loud in English. When all students are actively participating, a situation that we call **simultaneous participation**, our job becomes much easier. Students teach themselves, and we merely serve as a monitor or facilitator of students' learning.

PRINCIPLE 6: Individualization

In large classes, it's easy to treat your students as a collective rather than as individuals. Similar to principle 1 and in-line with the multiple intelligences idea of intrapersonal intelligence, good TEFL instructors provide opportunities for students to work on a solitary basis and to express themselves as individuals. Silence in the TEFL classroom is not always a negative; in fact, self-study and reflection can be one of the most positive signals that your students are acquiring the targeted language and skills you aim to teach. For these reasons, it is important to:

- give students time to work alone and reflect;
- have students keep a journal in which they can express personal thoughts only for you and themselves;
- give all students a chance to have input on class topics.

One of the keys to language learning is getting students to practice the target language outside of the classroom. There are several ways to accomplish this:

1. Assign homework.
2. Encourage students to keep an English diary or language learning journal.
3. Pair individual students with a conversation partner or pen pal.
4. Allow students to create individual research projects or projects where they practice English in a manner suitable to their personal needs and wants.
5. Conference with students individually on a regular basis.

PRINCIPLE 7: Open-endedness

English has the largest vocabulary of any language on Earth. It would be impossible to memorize or predict every conversation that your students will encounter in their lives. Rather, through their **combinatorial power** all languages allow for multiplicity of syntactical constructions, ideas, and expressions. Activities that allow students many possibilities for choosing appropriate language items are more authentic than activities that strive for a single correct answer.

Reflections: One of my biggest aggravations as a new TEFL instructor in China was getting my students to view English as a real, living language and not merely as something to memorize and repeat back on a test. A common example of this occurred whenever I greeted my students. "Hi, how are you?" I would ask. "Fine, thank you, and you?" 99.9% of my students would unvaryingly respond. Their responses were so automatic that I found it difficult to extend the conversation due to a sense of inauthenticity and de-personalization. Finally, I resolved to teach my students that there were various open-ended responses to "How are you?" and that this question was designed to initiate further small talk. "I'm tired / I'm happy / I'm angry / I'm sad / I'm excited / I'm nervous / I'm great / I'm ok / I'm in a hurry / I'm hungry / I'm energized / I'm bored because..." I left the responses open-ended because my main goal was for students to increase their fluency by speaking in fuller, more individualized, and more authentic ways. Then, I had trained students how to respond to an authentic statement with follow-up questions. "**Why** are you tired?" "**When** did you go to sleep? **Where** did you go last night? **Who** were you with?"

Suddenly, as I walked around the campus, I would notice students saying hello to each other and myself, making small talk in English for a few minutes rather than just saying, "I'm fine thank you and you?" and then rushing off before a response could be uttered. In other words, open-ended conversations in the targeted language began to become prevalent and students came to view English as an authentic, real-world tool rather than another classroom exercise to memorize and later forget. This was one of my proudest and greatest accomplishments during my first year teaching English!

Below are a few common activities that strive for open-endedness. Please discuss each one with a partner and consider how they aim for more fluent and authentic language use in the ESOL classroom.

- Sentence completion: "I want to improve my English because...", "It really bothers me when people..."
- Story completion / movie stop,
- Allow student to choose which questions to answer out of a given set,
- Brainstorming,
- Text paraphrasing,
- Posing questions which can be answered in many different ways.

PRINCIPLE 8: Routines

New lessons effectively build upon previous lessons. For this reason, from the very first day of class, I'm trying to establish certain routines that will help students to use English in more fluent, accurate, and complex ways throughout the entire year. You've seen this already in the previous principle, **open-endedness**, in which the teacher aims to establish a routine of giving and accepting open-ended responses to "Hi, how are you?" speaking in complete sentences, and asking follow-up questions. These techniques are designed to allow students to process English through their own minds and perceptions rather than relying solely upon the teacher to lead the conversation. Unfortunately, second language classrooms tend to establish certain routines and patterns that must be actively contradicted by a TEFL instructor with different goals and techniques. In other words, TEFL instructors must establish their own routines—making clear what is expected of the students and how the EFL class may differ from other classes by clearly explicating new routines and patterns. Establishing routines helps the class to operate smoothly and contributes to good classroom management.

Some common routines that new TEFL instructors may want to establish from the outset include:

- getting students to use their English names;
- speaking only in English when the TEFL instructor is in the room;
- placing nametags on the desk at the start of class;
- write out the day's activities on the board before the class arrives and check off the activities as the lesson progresses;

- post due-dates in a visible place in the classroom;
- assign students to distribute and collect papers;
- getting into groups of two, three, four, or five in a timely manner;
- counting off in English;
- speaking in complete sentences;
- asking follow-up questions;
- "Three before me" rule: When working in groups, students should ask three classmates an information question before asking the teacher.
- sitting down, opening textbooks to the correct page, locating paper and pencils in a timely manner;
- correcting partners' mistakes rather than relying on the teacher;
- teaching basic classroom English expressions (e.g., I'm sorry I don't understand, can you repeat that? Excuse me, can you write an example on the board? Can I join your group? I have to leave early today, is that ok? etc.).

Reflection and Activity for Teachers
1. Think of two additional routines that you would like to establish from the outset of your class.
2. Create an activity that will help to teach these two routines to your students. Discuss with a partner.

PRINCIPLE 9: Enlarging the Circle

Although it may be difficult to personalize a lesson plan for a large class of 60+ students, we should strive to try to include as many students into the conversation as possible. A teacher who expects and encourages class-wide participation keeps all students on their toes and active in their learning process. In order to enlarge the circle of participation, here are some simple steps to follow:

- Call on students in an unpredictable order. Don't call on the first person to raise their hand.
- Don't be afraid of silence.
- Have students call on each other.
- Stand away from a student who's speaking so his/her voice carries across the room.
- After posing a question to the class, allow some thinking time before students volunteer an answer.
- Listen carefully to students and allow student-initiated topics to interrupt the lesson.

Chapter 8 Nine Principles of TEFL

Reflection and Activity for Teachers

1. Without looking, what are the nine principles of TEFL? Explain each in your own words.
2. Take out one of your lesson plans. In groups, discuss whether or not each of the 9 Principles of TEFL is evident in this lesson plan (15 mins). For each principle that is evident, provide an example. For each principle that is not evident, provide a suggestion for revision.
3. What are the benefits of using this type of activity (group revision of pre-prepared material) in an EFL classroom? In what situation would you most likely use this type of activity? Can you think of how this type of activity might be adapted?

Former US Senator Fred Thompson with CTLC foreign teachers in China
前美国国会参议员 Fred Thompson 和 CTLC 外教

Classroom Management

Chapter 9

The goals for this chapter are:
- To get control of your teaching environment.
- To recognize potentially negative situations that could disrupt a class' learning and how to positively change them.
- To deal with troublesome student behaviors and interactions.

Classroom Management

One experienced instructor of children in the U.S. has a saying, "Don't smile before Christmas." In other words, a new teacher must continually (or at least for the first half of the school year) display a serious, stern, and professional demeanor in front of the classroom or he or she may be seen as "soft" or "easy to walk over" by the students. This instructor and many others believe that it is easier to loosen up the reigns once **routines** and expectations have been established than to befriend one's students from the very beginning and attempt to portray a serious, stern, and professional attitude later on. While I cannot argue that this approach may be effective for large classes of young public school children in American public schools, I can point out that there are significant differences to classroom management for TEFL courses in China.

There are two common approaches to classroom management: a) befriend your students or b) don't smile before Christmas. My own approach is somewhere in the middle of two extremes.

Chapter 9 Classroom Management

Students expect a certain level of professionalism and classroom management from their teacher, not a friend of the same age and interests. In fact, in my experience, the establishment of routines, appropriate lesson planning, and the preparedness of the teacher are the single largest predictors of classroom behavior. However, while lesson planning, preparation and establishing routines are signs of a professional TEFL instructor, so too are smiling, personalizing questions, varying activities from challenging and serious to light-hearted and fun, encouraging <u>all</u> students' participation, and treating students as equals with individual interests and ideas rather than as lessers whom we must control.

It's also important to recognize that the objectives of TEFL instruction in China may significantly alter how we approach classroom management. For example, consider:

1. The primary goal of TEFL instruction in China is to increase students' fluency by getting them to talk more and express their own ideas in open-ended, authentic ways.
2. Students, especially Chinese students, are naturally hesitant to speak in a second language in front of their peers. Creating a safe and comfortable environment in which students can practice English without fear of criticism or correction, directly contradicts the approach of "not smiling before Christmas."
3. The overwhelming majority of students are well-behaved, and repeated pronouncements against "bad behavior" often discourage an enlarged circle of participation.
4. Face-saving is an especially important aspect of Chinese culture that many Westerners fail to appreciate at first. What a TEFL teacher does in the name of reestablishing control of the classroom may be achieved at the expense of isolating or losing the face of individual or small groups of students. While the lesson may be saved, long-term resentment and a sense of separation from one's peers may develop and fester.
5. Rather than creating an appearance of serious professionalism, a teacher who doesn't smile may appear unhappy or unable to master his or her professional environment.

The reason why experienced TEFL instructors encounter fewer classroom behavior problems than new instructors is relatively simple. As the Buddhist monks say, "Whenever you point your finger at someone else, there are three fingers point right back at you." Experienced TEFL instructors take the time to reflect on how their own actions may affect the behavior of the classroom before singling out individual, unruly students. Experienced TEFL instructors learn to present themselves as a professional who comes to class prepared and able to help students achieve their personal goals for English language learning. When the lesson is effective, 90% of classroom management difficulties disappear. Moreover, experienced TEFL instructors act as models for effective language use: we are cool; we are interested in the world, and in communicating with people, especially with individual students who want to grow and learn. Krashen's theory of $i + 1$ may be directly applicable to classroom management. A teacher who shows a little more energy and excitement than his or her students is actually modeling effective classroom behavior. A teacher who wastes energy dictating students' behavior or trying to manage students' interactions in such a way beyond what they are willing or capable of doing is actually modeling poor classroom behavior. Students learn as much from how their teacher acts as from what he or she actually teaches. If you want to establish positive classroom behavior, start with yourself!

Be Positive: How a Lesson Is Learned

Many new TEFL instructors fail to appreciate the processes involved in second language acquisition. Hopefully, the first half of this textbook has given you a sufficient foundation to understand the importance of practice to acquiring an L2. As a teacher trainer, I follow this simple pattern:

1. Tell (10%)
2. Show (25%)
3. Practice (40%)
4. Directed Feedback (50%)
5. Practice with the Feedback (75%)
6. More Feedback (85%)
7. Teach Someone Else (100%)

The most common mistake I see with new teachers is their tendency to dominate the talking in the classroom. Remember: your English is fine; your students' English needs more practice. Try to limit your teacher talk and instructions before activities to 10% of the total amount of speaking that takes place in the classroom. One simple way to accomplish this task is to call on students to summarize the instructions you have given. Second, students may require a correct model before beginning an activity. As a TEFL teacher, proper modeling of what is expected during the activity can cut down on lengthy explanations and confusion. Students learn not only by listening but also by seeing. Third, practice. Give your students ample time to practice the targeted language or skill. Students will hopefully acquire more (roughly 40%) of a lesson if given one chance to practice. If students are given multiple chances to practice and provided with directed feedback from a peer, the teacher, or the class following each practice, their ability to acquire the targeted language or skill more than doubles (roughly 85%). Finally, don't let go of the reigns completely to put the responsibility for teaching, explaining the importance, or summarizing what was learned in the students' hands. The best way to learn something is to teach it to someone else, and when your students are able to teach the lesson to their peers then they will have truly acquired the targeted language and skill and you will have 60+ teachers rather than just one, thus making classroom management the responsibility of all rather than one.

Typical Issues for New Teachers

A comprehensive list of classroom management issues that new teachers encounter is offered below. As you read each one, try to think of several ways that you can overcome these common shortcomings and improve your teaching ability.

Chapter 9 Classroom Management

1. No clear learning objectives.
2. Overpraise students for doing what is expected.
3. Don't know the difference between praise and acknowledgement and when each is appropriate.
4. Fail to do effective long-range planning.
5. Spend too much time with one student or one group and do not monitor the entire class.
6. Begin a new activity before gaining the students' attention.
7. Talk too fast, and are sometimes shrill.
8. Use a voice level that is too loud or too soft, too fast or too slow.
9. Stand too long in one place.
10. Sit too long while teaching.
11. Overemphasize the negative.
12. Do not require students to raise hands and be acknowledged before responding.
13. Are way too serious and not much fun.
14. Are way too much fun and not serious.
15. Fall into a rut by using the same teaching strategy or combination of strategies day after day.
16. Are afraid of silence (wait time).
17. Are ineffective when they use facial expressions and body language.
18. Tend to talk to and interact with only half the class (usually their favorites, and usually on the right).
19. Spend large amounts of class time collecting or handing out students' work.
20. Interrupt students while they are on task.
21. Use "SHHHH" as a means of quieting students (one of the most annoying and ineffective behaviors).
22. Overuse verbal efforts to stop inappropriate student behavior—talk alone accomplishes little.
23. Settle for less rather than demand more.
24. Use threats to control the class (short-term: produces results; long-term: backfires).
25. Fail to do comprehension checks to see if students understand the content as it is taught.
26. Use poorly worded, ambiguous questions.
27. Try to talk over student noise (when you do, you lose and they win).
28. Are consistently inconsistent.
29. Will do anything to be liked by students.
30. Do not learn and use student names in an effective way (kids pick up quickly on this and respond in kind).
31. Permit students to be inattentive to media presentations.
32. Introduce too many topics simultaneously.

33. Take too much time to give verbal directions for an activity (an inability to focus and explain effectively).
34. Take too much time for an activity (usually the result of poor planning).
35. Overuse punishment for classroom misbehavior.

Common Scenarios

It would be impossible to list every problem you're likely to encounter over the next year of TEFL teaching in China. Here are a few that I have personally had to contemplate over the past 12 years of my TEFL career. While there may be no 100% right or wrong responses to these scenarios, there are some responses that will likely produce better results than others. Please discuss each scenario and how you would respond. Then, compare your response to those of a more experienced TEFL instructor. This may be a good opportunity to get to know your trainers better and learn from their experiences.

Scenario 1: A student at the back of the room has her head down and is not participating with her group.

Scenario 2: A student in the middle continually translates everything you say into Chinese. When students with lower-level English struggle, this student translates their Chinese into English so that you can more easily understand them.

Scenario 3: Several male students are insulting a female student calling her names like "pig."

Scenario 4: Your lesson plans are going well for all of your classes except one. This class continues to show less interest and possess lower English abilities than your other classes and you are noticing more classroom behavior problems, namely lack of interest and motivation.

Scenario 5: Using your teacher face and stern voice, you direct to a student to open his book, pay attention, and speak English only. He ignores you and continues to speak in Chinese with his partner.

Scenario 6: Although you didn't see who did it, one student threw a paper airplane at you while you were writing on the board. Many students laughed.

Scenario 7: You've asked your students to bring a newspaper article in English to class, but only a handful of the students have done the homework.

Scenario 8: You're at your wits' end. One student is openly mocking you and disobeying your instructions. This has occurred several times and you've already spoken in private with the student.

Be Positive: Don't Jump to Conclusions

In the above scenarios, did you reflect first upon your own responsibility in the situation? Or did you jump directly to how to punish the student and maintain your control of the class? It's hard for us to take responsibility for our own shortcomings, especially when we are older and wiser,

Chapter 9 Classroom Management

and place the blame on those younger and less mature than us. But who do we expect more maturity and wisdom from: the teacher or the child? If we are not reflective and caring in our own actions, how can we expect those much younger and less experienced than us to display caring, self-reflective behavior?

> **A Real Scenario**: When I first began teaching TEFL to young children, I encountered classroom management problems similar to the ones above and more. I remember in particular one girl who had her head down at the back of the class and refused to participate. I immediately jumped to the punishment phase. This student was directly questioning my authority and her behavior if left unpunished would spread to the other students around her. Soon there would be anarchy and I would lose control of my students. I tapped her on the shoulder and sternly instructed her to open her book. She refused to respond. I glowered down upon her and raised my voice. Still, she did not respond. I physically opened her book and placed it inches away from her eyes. Still, she did not respond. I attempted to lift her head. Still, she did not respond. I berated her, flicked her ear, and told her to leave my classroom. Finally, she left and I felt victorious as the other students in the classroom whispered under their breath. What I hadn't realized was that this student's grandmother had just died and that she was in such a depressed mood that she was unable to study that day. Her actions were not a personal attack on me or my teaching, but on factors outside of the classroom and beyond my control. I felt like an insensitive moron! Moreover, I'd lost face where I thought I was saving face. All because I hadn't checked my assumptions and had jumped to a false conclusion.

The above scenario could have been easily resolved with patience, positivity, and professionalism. Rather than jump to the punishment, I've learned a more positive way to handle potential behavior problems.

1) **Investigate**—Ask the student how he or she feels or the reason behind his or her perceived inappropriate actions. Maybe you have misread the situation and need more information.

2) **Negotiate/Offer support**—Rather than dictate your will, try to negotiate or lend support. For example, a student may refuse to participate in a group discussion because one of the group partners is at odds that day with the student. Moving her to another group may be more productive than fighting her to participate in her original group.

3) **Let small things slide**—Laughter in the classroom is not the end of the world even it comes at your expense; in fact, laughter and small acting outs can often release tension. If students are still learning and the lesson is still moving, there is no need to stop the momentum to draw attention to small mistakes. Note: letting things slide is not the same as ignoring them. It's important to keep a mental or physical record of behavioral issues in case they repeat and become more serious.

4) **Give second chances**—If a student's behavior improves, acknowledge the improvement.

Encourage and reward students' positive interactions more than you punish their negative interactions.

5) **Do not stop the majority of students' learning to punish the minority**—You can acknowledge inappropriate behavior when it occurs but confront the behavior at a time and manner of your choosing. Ultimately, you are responsible for the management of classroom interactions.

6) **Conserve your voice and your police face**—Screaming and playing the role of "bad cop" is an ineffective way to deal with large classrooms. Most of the students are well-behaved and do not need to be threatened or punished into appropriate classroom behavior. A consistent scowl or commandments to behave better are wasted upon the majority of students. Therefore, conserve your teacher face and teacher voice for those who truly deserve it and only when it is needed. This may involve asking students to stay after class when you can confront them without hurting them or you losing face.

7) **Be responsible and positive**—A teacher who cannot control his or her classroom is not highly regarded by other teachers. Never let your students see you sweat. If you walk out the classroom cursing and angry, your students' view of you will never change. If you cannot positively interact with a child through reasoning and encouragement, then you are the child. While new teachers may need the support of others, more experienced teachers at times; this support cannot always be counted upon and may erode students' confidence in the teacher's abilities.

8) **Think before you act**—It's natural to make mistakes, but it's crazy to take the same approach and expect different results. Reflect on the problem and how you dealt with it. Reflect on the context (i.e., your own teaching strategies and lesson plans) that may have led to the problem. Think about how you can change *your* actions to create a more positive, safe environment for all.

Reward Good Behavior

A better way of managing the classroom is to reward students when their actions and participation is positive. How are students to know what your definition for "good" classroom behavior is if you only punish "bad" classroom behavior? Rewarding good student behavior is a more positive approach to classroom management. There are several approaches experienced teachers will use to reward good behavior: grades, individual or class points, stickers, candy, or teacher dollars to be redeemed for prizes. Examples of student behavior worthy of reward may include:

- a student who helps teach the lesson to a struggling student,
- a student whose work goes above and beyond your expectations,
- a student who asks questions and challenges you to become a better teacher,
- a student who changes his/her behavior to reflect your suggestions,

Chapter 9 Classroom Management

- a student who volunteers or goes first,
- a student who leads—without dominating—discussions,
- a student who assists the teacher,
- a student who uses English outside of the classroom.

Reflection and Activity for Teachers

1. Practice your teacher face and teacher voice with your partner. Only one word should be needed.
2. In a small group discuss: What are some classroom management problems you have already encountered? How would you suggest a new teacher deal with these problems?
3. Establishing routines from the first day of class can curtail future classroom behavior issues. What are some routines that you could introduce to your students in the first few weeks that may alleviate behavior issues in the future? Share your responses with another group.

CTLC national coordinator Dawn Byres teaches a training class
CTLC 外教领队 Dawn Bares 在国家外专局培训外教

Teaching Primary School

Chapter 10

The goals for this chapter are:
- To create TEFL lessons plans of interest to young learners.
- To use multiple intelligence to vary activities around a single theme or language objective.
- To create materials appropriate to young learners.

Create Interest

Young children are natural inquisitive and interested in their surroundings. Unfortunately, most language learning classrooms are not naturally attractive or interesting to young learners. Colors, personalized posters, maps, photos, show and tell objects, music, games, drawing, and constructions can help to enliven a gray, monotonous classroom. Likewise, an interesting and interested teacher can help to enliven young students learning. In line with the idea of $i + 1$, new TEFL teachers of young children will often discover that the energy level and interest level is so high that the teacher's energy and interest must correspondingly rise. While some find this tiring on a yearly basis, teachers of young children surely find this to be one of the most rewarding aspects of their jobs. Hopefully, you will be able to test your personality before a group of young learners before deciding if this could be a chosen career path for you.

Luckily, we were young school children once upon a time and have probably interacted with young learners at some point in our lives. We can predict what young children will be interested in and what they will not be interested in. I sometimes say that the best teacher for a 6-year-old child is not a 30-year-old linguistic professor who speaks as such, but a teacher who can act and speak like a 7-year-old (see *i + 1*). As a teacher of young children, we need to remember our audience. What is interesting to us may not be of interest to our students. Likewise, our language abilities may far supersede those of our young learners. Good teaching meets the needs and wants of the students. And this is no more prevalent than in primary school TEFL instruction.

Two Conflicting Approaches: Eclecticism versus GTM

Content-Based vs. Grammar Based
Production vs. Reception
Connected Learning vs. Memorization
Scaffolded Teaching vs. Scattered Topics
Outside Learning vs. Classroom Learning
Intrinsic Motivation vs. Extrinsic Motivation

All of the preceding chapters on language acquisition and lesson planning are relevant to the teaching of young children in TEFL. What differs are the targeted students' interests, attention spans, and language abilities. One essential difference to effective TEFL instruction of young learners is the pacing of the lesson. You've probably noticed that children become bored more easily than adults; moreover, they constantly seek out new games or activities that spark their interests. They are open-minded, willing to take risks, and unafraid of making mistakes, especially in speaking a second language. Luckily, these qualities match nicely with the idea of **multiple intelligences** and an eclectic versus a more repetitively, structured **GTM**-type approach to language teaching.

If we remember the seven multiple intelligences:

1. Linguistic
2. Mathematical/Logical
3. Spatial/Visual
4. Musical
5. Bodily/Kinesthetic
6. Interpersonal
7. Intrapersonal

We can easily begin to create eclectic lesson plans that center around targeted language tasks or skills. For example, imagine we our teaching a primary school class about the days of the week. We could have them read a short story about the days of the week (linguistic); we could have them create a daily plan for how they spend each day of their week (logic), we could have them draw pictures of what they do each day (visual); we could sing a song about the days of the week (musical); we could play charades and invite student to act out how they spend their time during particular days of the week (bodily/kinesthetic); we could have them compare their daily activities with a partner (interpersonal); we could ask them to show and tell their parents' daily habits via a videotaped personal diary (intrapersonal). If we relegate 5—10 minutes for each of these activities, we have created an interesting and eclectic 50-minute lesson plan that may not hold all students' attention for all the time, but may hold most students' attention for most of the time. Moreover, through eclectic approaches to the same theme, we can nearly guarantee that students will have acquired the targeted language (in this case, days of the week) and can produce the language in the next lesson.

Connected Learning

Like a spider's web, we actually strengthen the core of our lesson through eclectic extensions and connections. Note: if we were just playing games or filing time (a common mistake of untrained, unprofessional TEFL teachers) our lessons would appear disconnected to our students, and we'd have to rely solely upon the entertainment value of the games to create interest rather than the intrinsic motivation that all young learners have for communicating more clearly and effectively.

The goal of teaching young children should therefore be exactly thesame as teaching adults: to acquire English in a systematic and naturalway. Although games can be fun and raise the interest level of young learners, learning a language through other intelligences can be just as fun and interesting. Young learners do not protest against effective teaching that connects language and strategies in a clear manner.

Young learners enjoy the challenge of learning a new language and communicating with people from foreign cultures. I cannot, however, guarantee that young learners will always enjoy the same games and activities. Therefore, I strongly encourage that new TEFL instructors concentrate first on the language and skill goals of their lessons before implementing games. Remember: you are now a teacher, not an entertainer! Learning can be just as fun for your students—and even more rewarding in the long-term—than playing games!

Chapter 10 Teaching Primary School

Scaffolding Lessons

Just as with all lesson planning, good TEFL lessons for primary school students build upon previously acquired input and learning. You want to reflect on what students have already learned and how you can **scaffold** new material from the old material.

Ultimately, scaffolding will help to organize your teaching, making English acquisition easier for your students and, as a result, you will be heralded as a more effective teacher. While we praise the use of eclecticism in the classroom, teachers of young learners especially need to establish **routines** that will quickly scaffold into greater productivity and intrinsic motivation of the young learners. Some routines you may want to initiate in the primary school TEFL classroom include:

1. Writing the target language or skills focus on the board.
2. Listing the planned activities and crossing them out as the lesson progresses.
3. Reviewing or repeating previous day's lesson at the start of the next day's lesson. This is a routine warm-up activity used by many experienced TEFL instructors of young children.
4. Pointing out and reminding students of how new material builds upon previous material.
5. Occasionally quizzing or questioning students on previous material to ensure the language is acquired and not memorized.
6. Asking students to summarize the lesson and demonstrate how it can be used to extend material from previous lessons at the end of class.

A Simple Teaching Process for Primary School TEFL

In my limited experience teaching English to young children, I developed my own routine which has helped me to create a more structured classroom while at the same time encouraging eclectic approaches and appealing to the strengths of young learners. Here's the outline of my routine:

1. Create Interest
2. Introduce New Concept
3. Read Aloud & Track
4. Word Gesture & Picture Clues

5. Read & Chime
6. Post-Reading Activity

Unfortunately, most young learners do not come to class ready to learn. They have not chosen to learn English and may not recognize its relevance to their futures. In other words, they lack intrinsic motivation in comparison with adult learners who self-select to study a second language. Therefore, the first step in my process is to create interest and prepare students for the lesson. Fortunately, creating interest in young learners is a relatively easy process. Singing a song, playing a game, acting out via TPR, moving around the room, or even reviewing the previous lesson are examples of **warm-up activities** geared toward creating interest in young learners for studying English. It's important to remember to keep these warm-up activities short and to-the-point. A warm-up activity that goes on for too long can create negative effects in students' **intrinsic motivation** for learning English. The goal of a good warm-up activity is to create interest in the lesson plan and get students ready for classroom learning.

Now that students are warmed-up and I have their attention, I need to clearly introduce what the target language or skill for today's lesson will be. Hopefully, this lesson will **scaffold** from the previous lesson and students' level of interest will increase rather than diminish. Writing the target language clearly on the board can help direct students' attention back to the new concept when their attentions start to wonder.

Young learners often do not possess the vocabulary and syntax to produce long, meaningful spoken or written language. They are strongly **receptive** learners (focus on reading and listening) rather than **productive** learners (focus on speaking and writing). This tendency is natural and in accordance with Krashen's predictions. Therefore, a good deal of time should be spent on building young learners' vocabulary and getting them to speak and write in simple complete sentences (although later, you will want to **scaffold** upon these simple sentence so that students begin to produce longer, complex sentences and vocabulary). Teaching students how to read phonetically in English and **track** below each word or phoneme with their index finger enables faster word recognition and stronger reading skills. A second reading using flashcards, picture clues, and/or word gestures can further reinforce new vocabulary and concepts in young learners' minds. A third reading requiring students to fill in gaps or long pauses in the teacher's reading, thus **producing** short segments of the targeted language in their own speech further **connects** the new concept in young learners' minds and encourages them toward **production**.

Now that students have read/heard and acquired the new concept through eclectic yet connected activities, it's time to have fun and extend the lesson with a post-reading activity. A **post-reading activity** could be a song that uses some of the words from the text (musical intelligence); it could be an art project in which students draw a poster that illustrates the new concept (visual intelligence); it could be a bulls-eye game that requires one team to ask a question and the other team to respond using the new concept accurately before throwing the ball at the target (interpersonal intelligence); it could be to act out the reading (bodily/kinesthetic intelligence), or it could be to complete some exercise in the workbook (intrapersonal and linguistic intelligence). Regardless of which activity you decide upon, it should: (1) appeal to the students' personal interests, (2) connect to the targeted language or skill from the day's lesson, and (3) be eclectic and different from the prior day's activities. As time goes by, classes will develop favorite games or activities, and you can repeat these favorites (or hold them as a reward for good behavior) simply by adapting them to a new targeted language or skill focus. Over the years, experienced TEFL instructors of young children begin to collect effective activities and to share them with other instructors. You can find many of these ideas in this book and on our list serve. Even better though is to take time to talk with the teachers around you, to share effective lessons plans and activities of your own, and to borrow new idea from your peers. Of course, a little thanks and feedback from the lessons you borrow is welcome if not required.

Sample Lessons for Young Learners

Grade: Primary 1
Time: 50 minutes
Language Goal: days of the week
Vocabulary : Monday, Tuesday, Wednesday, Thursday, Friday, Saturday, Sunday
Review : Numbers 1—10
Materials Needed : paper, pens, "One Monday Morning"

    1a.   Create Interest :

Monday	Tuesday	Wednesday	Thursday	Friday	Saturday	Sunday
		1	2	3	4	5
6	7	8	9	10	11	12
13	14	15	16	17	18	19
20	21	22	23	24	25	26

    Option 1: Teacher reads a number and students respond in chorus with the corresponding day of the week.

    Option 2: Students count in turn and supply the corresponding day of the week (e.g., one Wednesday, two Thursday). To make it harder you could practice even numbers or multiples (e.g., four Saturday, eight Wednesday).

    Option 3: Teacher places seven pieces of paper with the days of the week throughout the classroom. Teacher then calls a number and students have to touch the corresponding paper. The last student to touch the correct paper is out.

    1b. Create Interest (Alternative Warm-Up Activity):

Monday	Tuesday	Wednesday	Thursday	Friday	Saturday	Sunday

Teacher models a corresponding gesture for each day of the week and practices the gestures with the students. Then, teacher prompts, "Show me what you do on Thursday." "Show me what you do on Monday." Students respond in chorus with the correct gestures. Finally, students take turns calling out the days of the week and asking students to respond with their own gestures. Students can draw pictures of activities they perform on Saturday and Sundays.

2. *Introduce New Concept*: Today's Lesson—Days of the Week

Monday, Tuesday, Wednesday, Thursday, Friday, Saturday, Sunday (written on board)

3. *Read Aloud & Track*: Teacher reads the story aloud while the students track, moving their index finger below the spoken word. There are several story and children's books that introduce the days of the week. One example is *One Monday Morning* by Uri Shulevitz: "On Friday, the king, the queen, the prince, the knight, and the little dog came to visit me. But I wasn't home." Although some words may be new and difficult for students, remember the focus is on the days of the week and reading phonetically not all learning all the names for a king's entourage.

4. *Word Gestures & Picture Clues*: Teacher reads the story a second time while the students gesture or hold up pictures when they hear the corresponding word.

5. *Read & Chime*: Teacher reads the story a third time with long pauses inviting students to fill-in-the-blanks in unison or individually. Teacher pauses and expectations should be based upon students' levels and prior knowledge. Eventually, students are now reading parts of the story aloud to each other without the teacher's prompts.

6a. *Post-Reading Activity*: Sing a Song

With the teacher's help, students sing the following song acting out the various lyrics.

Here We Go 'Round the Mulberry Bush

Here we go 'round the mulberry bush
The mulberry bush, the mulberry bush
Here we go 'round the mulberry bush
So early Monday morning.
This is the way we wash our clothes (Tuesday)
This is the way we scrub the floor (Wednesday)
This is the way we bake the bread (Thursday)
This is the way we sit and rest (Sunday)

6b: Draw a Picture: Students ask each other about the activities they perform on certain days of the week and draw a picture in the corresponding blank space.

Monday	Tuesday	Wednesday	Thursday	Friday	Saturday	Sunday

Conclusion: Teacher quizzes students before they can leave the classroom on the days of the week.

- What day is today?
- What day is tomorrow?
- What day was yesterday?

Extension: In the next class, we will learn how to tell time. Therefore, I will expect students to be able to produce speech like, "On Tuesday at nine am, I swim." Or "On Saturday at midnight, I sleep."

Here's another sample lesson plan from Gwyn Lewis, a CTLC 2009-2011 teacher.

Grade: Primary 3

Time: 40 minutes

Topic: Goldilocks and the Three Bears

Language Goal: Students will be able to write a simple story through writing dialogue and master the too construction.

Grammar/Sentence Pattern: too hot, too cold, too big, too small, too hard, too soft, just right, dialogue/script format

New Vocabulary: bowl, porridge, just right, broke

Review: bear, mommy, daddy, baby, big, small, hard, soft, hot, chair, bed

Materials Needed: internet, ppt, flashcards, paper and pens (students should have and paper)

Warm-Up: How are you? Teacher asks "How are you? Why?" Students answer. After a few times, teacher steals student's chair and student becomes the teacher, asking "How are you? Why?"

Activity 1: Watch Goldilocks story on www.britishcouncil.org/kids. Kids repeat each line on screen.

Activity 2: Flash cards: Goldilocks, Daddy Bear, Mommy Bear, Baby Bear, Too hot! Too cold! Just right. Too big! Too big too! Broke too hard! Too soft! Practice flashcards with whole class

Activity 3: Our story. Using ppt, students retell the story in dialogue form. Goldilocks: I'm hungry! This is too hot, etc. Once the class understands, they are invited to start changing details (Teacher says "Oh no! Is this our story? No, this is the computer story! In our story, maybe there are three lions? In our story maybe Goldilocks is a boy?") Continue with activity until the class understands they can change anything, the sillier the better.

Activity 4: Your story. Groups of 4. Groups rewrite the end of the story in dialogue form with the option of changing any detail they want. Teacher helps with vocabulary and encourages creativity. Groups who finish early can make masks.

Conclusion : Select groups perform story with a fifth person.

Extension : Fairy Tale continues into next two lessons introducing Little Red Riding Hood. Students put together cut up script of Goldilocks, watch the Little Red Riding Hood story, in groups of four memorize printed copies of the script and perform it for the class.

> **Reflection and Activity for Teachers**
>
> 1. What do you think of the sample lesson plans for young learners above? Which is designed for lower-level students? Which is designed for higher-level students? How would you adapt these lessons for the students you aim to teach?
> 2. List qualities that a good primary school should possess. Compare and contrast your list with that of a partner. Which of these qualities do you possess?
> 3. What are some differences involved in teaching TEFL to young learners compared to older learners? How can you adapt to teaching to compensate for these differences?

Former Shenzhen vice-mayor Zhuang Xinyi with CTLC faculties

Reading and Vocabulary

Chapter 11

The goals for this chapter are:
- To learn active reading strategies to enhance comprehension.
- To learn methods for vocabulary building.
- To improve and adjust reading rates.

Active Reading

How did you first learn to read? My father taught me to read phonetically, sounding out each letter and its corresponding sound. Over time, I began to read longer words, words I had never seen before, even made-up words which didn't appear in the dictionary. I read without the aid of my parents or a teacher because I possessed the necessary skills to read anything (in English) that I came across. I grew to enjoy reading in my free time. I read vociferously and actively. How did this happen? Was I naturally gifted? I don't think so. Simply put, I was taught how to read the right way.

The "right" way to read is to read actively. Reading is inherently connected to academic success. The table below highlights the strategies employed by successful readers:

Active Readers...	Passive Readers...
Tailor their reading to suit each assignment.	Read all assignments the same way.
Analyze the purpose of an assignment.	Read an assignment because it was assigned.
Adjust their speed to suit their purpose.	Read everything at the same speed.
Question ideas in the text.	Accept whatever is in print as true.
Make guesses and predictions as they read.	Read.
Compare and connect textbook material with lecture or other material.	Study lecture notes, the textbook, and handouts separately. Fail to connect materials.
Skim heading to find out what an assignment is about before beginning to read.	Check the length of an assignment and then begin reading.
Make sure they understand what they are reading as they go along.	Read until the assignment is completed.
Read with pencil in hand, highlighting, jotting notes, and marking key vocabulary.	Read.
Develop personalized strategies for reading.	Follow routine, standard methods. Read all assignments the same way.

* Adapted from McWhorter, K.T. (2007). *Reading Across Disciplines*, 3rd edition. New York: Pearson Longman.

Second Language Reading

As we have already seen, significant differences exist for L2 learners versus L1 learners. Some of the differences should be easy to recognize: (1) L1 readers tend to read more extensively in the target language than L2 readers; (2) L2 readers may possess different cultural assumptions and knowledge bases than L1 readers (e.g., a story about eating a cheesesteak sandwich while watching *American Idol* may be more comprehensible to some readers than others); (3) L2 readers may be unaware of how language changes according to genre and audience (e.g., academic register v. social register); (4) reading proficiency thresholds are generally lower for L2 than L1 readers due to unfamiliarity with vocabulary and syntax; (5) L2 readers tend to read slower than L1 readers.

Schema Theory

Anderson and Pearson (1984) are regarded as two of the forefathers of **schema theory** in ESOL reading. Similar to the idea of **scaffolding**, **schema theory** implies that prior knowledge is essential for the understanding of new knowledge. Before students read a text, teachers either need to: (1) help students build the prerequisite knowledge, or (2) remind them of what they already know before introducing new material. You're probably familiar with the idea of schema theory from your own reading classes. The introduction of new vocabulary, questions for discussion, visual aids, cultural/historical explanations, etc. before reading a new text helps to prepare the reader for the content within.

As reading involves not only language but also contextualized background knowledge, it is important to teach general knowledge and generic concepts that may unfamiliar to readers from other cultures. A large proportion of learner difficulties can be traced to insufficient general knowledge, especially in cross-cultural situations. Many L2 readers do not have the cultural background necessary to understand implications of text. Teachers must help learners build schemata and make connections between ideas. Discussion, songs, role play, illustrations, visual aids, and explanations of how a piece of knowledge applies are some of the techniques used to strengthen connections. Making connections to previous knowledge is how acquisition and learners takes place. **Schema theory** predicts that new input is mapped against existing schema and all aspects of that schema must be compatible with input information. Learners may become conflicted if the new material does graph onto their previous suppositions and schemata. Students' schemata will grow as new information is acquired, enabling them to become more independent and more active readers. Reader schema can be broken into two aspects: (1) formal schemata: background knowledge of the formal, rhetorical organizational structures of different types of texts, and (2) content schemata: background knowledge of the content area of the text (Carrell, 1983).

Unfortunately, deep-seated schemata are hard to change. An individual will often prefer to live with inconsistencies rather than to change a deeply-held value or belief. Teachers need to understand and be sympathetic to this tension. You can ease the difficulty students experience reading new material by teaching reading as a three-step process: (1) pre-reading, (2) through reading, and (3) post-reading.

- ■ **Pre-reading**: Discussion questions to activate schema, visual aids, graphic organizers, lectures, visual aids, demonstrations, role-play, text previewing, introduction and discussion of key vocabulary, and key-word/key-concept association activities. For example, showing pictures of a country before reading a text about that country or showing a clip from the movie before reading the novel.
- ■ **Through Reading**: Questions to find answers to, problem to solve through the reading, reading in chunks with discussion, questions between each chunk to ensure comprehension.

■ **Post-reading**: Discussion questions, re-telling, acting out the story, writing assignment, comprehension questions, and vocabulary exercises.

Organizational Patterns

Most texts follow a predictable pattern that students should be made aware of. By recognizing typical patterns of organizations, readers can better anticipate the author's arguments and explanations. Moreover, pattern recognition enhances memory and information recall (McWhorter, 2007). Finally, organizational patterns are most useful in organizing and expressing students' own ideas in speech or writing. Below is a chart of some of the most common organizational patterns in readings:

PATTERN	CHARACTERISTICS	TRANSITIONS
Definition	Explains the meaning of a word or phrase	Is, refers to, can be defined as, means, consists of, involves, is a term that, is called, is characterized by, occurs when, are those that, entails, corresponds to, is literally
Classification	Divides a topic into parts based on shared characteristics	Classified as, comprises, is composed of, several varieties of, different stages of, different groups that, includes, one, first, second, another, finally, last
Chronological Order	Describes events, processes, procedures	First, second, later, before, next, as soon as, after, then, finally, meanwhile, following, last, during, in, on, when, until
Process	Describes the order in which things are done or how things work	First, second, next, then, following, after that, last, finally
Order of Importance	Describes ideas in order of priority or preference	Less, more, primary, first, next, last, most important, primarily, secondarily
Spatial Order	Describes physical location or position in space	Above, below, beside, next to, in front of, behind, inside, outside, opposite, within, nearby

Chapter 11 Reading and Vocabulary

Cause and Effect	Describes how one or more things cause or are related to another	*Causes*: because (of), for, since, stems from, one cause is, one reason is, leads to, causes, creates, yields, produces, due to, breeds, for this reason *Effects*: consequently, results in, one result is, therefore, thus, as a result, hence
Comparison and Contrast	Discusses similarities and/or differences among ideas, theories, concepts, objects, or persons	*Similarities*: both, also, similarly, like, likewise, too, as well as, resembles, correspondingly, in the same way, to compare, in comparison, share *Differences*: unlike, differs from, in contrast, on the other hand, instead, despite, nevertheless, however, in spite of, whereas, as opposed to
Listing/Enumeration	Organizes lists of information: characteristics, features, parts, or categories	The following, several, for example, for instance, one, another, also, too, in other words, first, second, numerals (1, 2), letters (a, b), most important, the largest, the least, finally
Statement and Clarification	Indicates that information explaining an idea or concept will follow	In fact, in other words, clearly, evidently, obviously
Summary	Indicates that a condensed review of an idea or piece of writing is to follow	In summary, in conclusion, in brief, to summarize, to sum up, in short, on the whole
Generalization and Example	Provides examples that clarify a broad, general statement	For example, for instance, that is, to illustrate, thus
Addition	Indicates that additional information will follow	Furthermore, additionally, also, besides, further, in addition, moreover, again

* Adapted from McWhorter, K.T. (2007). *Reading Across Disciplines*, 3rd edition. New York: Pearson Longman.

Thinking Maps

As many students are visual learners, thinking maps have become a popular tool in the TEFL reading classroom. **Thinking maps** teach students how to recognize organizational partners within a text and increase their reading comprehension. Below are several examples of various thinking maps:

Purpose	Map Type
Defining in Context	Circle Map
Describing Qualities	Bubble Map
Comparing and Contrasting	Double Bubble Map
Classifying	Tree Map
Part-Whole	Brace Map
Sequencing	Flow Chart
Cause and Effect	Multi-flow Chart
Analogies	Bridge Map

Reading Strategies

There are several strategies that can be taught in the ESOL reading class to ensure greater comprehension. These include but are not limited to:

Chapter 11 Reading and Vocabulary

- Preparing to read
- Previewing: Skimming and scanning
- Using context clues
- Learning prefixes, roots, and suffixes
- Identifying thesis, main ideas, and supporting ideas
- Recognizing typical organizational patterns
- Making inferences
- Differentiating fact from opinion
- Isolating author's purpose/tone/bias/quality of evidence
- Connotations
- Highlighting
- Annotating
- Paraphrasing
- Outlining
- Mapping
- Evaluating sources
- Adjusting reading rates
- Summarizing
- Predicting
- Clarifying
- Asking questions
- Connecting
- Evaluating
- Checking for answers

- Translating
- Preparing to read
- Previewing: Skimming and scanning
- Using context clues
- Learning prefixes, roots, and suffixes
- Identifying thesis, main ideas, and supporting ideas
- Recognizing typical organizational patterns
- Making inferences
- Differentiating fact from opinion
- Isolating author's purpose/tone/bias/quality of evidence
- Connotations
- Highlighting
- Annotating
- Paraphrasing
- Outlining
- Mapping
- Evaluating sources
- Adjusting reading rates
- Summarizing
- Predicting
- Clarifying
- Asking questions
- Checking for answers
- Translating

Vocabulary: What is a morpheme?

Morphemes are the smallest unit of meaningful language. Prefixes (e.g. un-), suffixes (e.g., -able), and roots (e.g. geo) cannot stand alone yet convey meaning to the reader. For example, the morpheme -s implies plurality, signaling a difference in meaning between *dog* and *dogs*. Below are lists of some of the most common morphemes in the English language, which can be taught explicitly to your students.

PREFIX	MEANING	SAMPLE WORD
a-	not	asymmetrical
ab-	away	absent

ad-	toward	adhesive
ante-/pre-	before	antecedent/premarital
anti-	against	antiwar
bi-/di-/du-	two	bimonthly/divorce/duet
centi-	hundred	centigrade
circum-/peri-	around	circumference/perimeter
com-/col-/con-	with, together	compile/collide/convene
contra-/counter-	against	contradict
de-	away, from	depart
dec-/deci-	ten	decimal
dia-	through	diameter
dis-	apart, away, not	disagree
equi-	equal	equidistant
ex-/extra-	from, out of, former	ex-wife/extramarital
homo-	same	homogenized
hyper-	over, excessive	hyperactive
in-/il-/ir-/im-	not	incorrect/illogical/ irreversible/ impossible
inter-	between	interpersonal
intro-/intra-/in-	within, into, in	introduction
mal-	poorly, wrongly	malnourished
mega-	large	megaphone
micro-	small	microscope
milli-	thousand	milligram
mis-	wrongly	misunderstand
mono-/uni-	one	monocle/unicycle
multi-/poly-	many	multipurpose/polygon
nano-	extremely small	nanoplankton
non-	not	nonfiction
post-	after	posttest
pre-	before	preview
pseudo-	false	pseudoscientific
quad-	four	quadrant
quint-/pent-	five	quintet/pentagon
re-	back, again	review
retro-	backward	retrospect
semi-	half	semicircle
sub-	under, below	submarine
super-	above, extra	supercharge
tele-	far	telescope
trans-	cross, over	transcontinental
tri-	three	triangle
un-	not	unpopular

SUFFIX	SAMPLE WORD
Suffixes that refer to a state, condition or quality	
-able	touchable
-ance	assistance
-ation	confrontation
-ence	reference
-ible	tangible
-ic	chronic
-ion	discussion
-ish	girlish
-ity	superiority
-ive	permissive
-less	hopeless
-ment	amazement
-ness	kindness
-ous	jealous
-ty	loyalty
-y	creamy
Suffixes that mean "one who"	
-an/-ian	italian
-ant	participant
-ee	referee
-eer	engineer
-ent	resident
-er	teacher
-ist	activist
-or	advisor
Suffixes that mean "pertaining to or referring to"	
-ac	cardiac
-al	autumnal
-ary	secondary
-ship	friendship
-hood	brotherhood
-ward	homeward

COMMON ROOT	MEANING	SAMPLE WORD
anthropo	human being	anthropology
archaeo	ancient or past	archaeology
aster/astro	star	astronaut
aud/audit	hear	audible
bene	good, well	benefit
bio	life	biology
cap	take, seize	captive

cardi	heart	cardiology
chron(o)	time	chronology
corp	body	corpse
cred	believe	incredible
predict	dict/dic	tell, say
introduce	duc/duct	lead
factory	fact/fac	make, do
telegraph	graph	write
geophysics	geo	earth
gynecology	gyneco	woman
psychology	log/logo/logy	study, thought
permit/dismiss	mit/miss	send
immortal	mort/mor	die, death
neurology	neuro	nerve
sympathy	path	feeling
telephone	phono	sound, voice
photosensitive	photo	light
transport	port	carry
pulmonary	pulmo	lungs
microscope	scop	seeing
inscription	scrib/script	write
insensitive	sen/sent	feel
retrospect	spec/spic/spect	look, see
tension	tend/tent/tens	stretch or strain
territory	terr/terre	land, earth
theology	theo	god
convention	ven/vent	come
invert	vert/vers	turn
invisible/video	vis/vid	see
vocation	voc	call

Vocabulary: What is a "word"?

The lexicon (vocabulary) of the English language is comprised of thousands of words. But what is a word? Single words like *dog* are easy. But what about *motor home, put up with, right-of-way,* or *make hay while the sun shines,* are these separate words, one word, or something entirely different? Rather than words, linguists use the term lexical items which include:

- ■ Slang (e.g., *tight/cool* v. *good*)
- ■ Idioms (e.g., *over the hill*; *paint the town red*)
- ■ Proverbs (e.g., *Early to bed and early to rise makes a man healthy, wealth, and wise*).
- ■ Collocations (e.g., *adhere to; motion toward*)

Chapter 11 Reading and Vocabulary

Your students will want to know the lexicon most common in everyday English speech and writing. They may also want to know the lexicon necessary for their future careers or academic success. I strongly encourage high school students to bring—and use—a dictionary in the classroom. Some useful references for the teaching of lexicon not likely to be found in students' dictionaries include:

http://www.idiomconnection.com/, http://www.learn-english-today.com/idioms/idioms_proverbs.html, http://www.learn-english-today.com/Proverbs/proverbs.html, http://www.world-english.org/proverbs.htm, http://www.englishclub.com/vocabulary/collocations.htm, and http://www.peevish.co.uk/slang/.

Teaching Vocabulary

Lexicon instruction can be divided into three typical methods:

- ■ Incidental Learning: Extensive reading and listening (intermediate and advanced learners)
- ■ Explicit Instruction: Diagnosing words, presenting them, elaborating, developing fluency (beginning and intermediate learners)
- ■ Independent Strategy Development: Guessing from context and training learners to use dictionaries (all learners)

Obviously the more students read, the more vocabulary they will **incidentally** acquire. **Extensive reading** encourages students to read large amounts of diverse material in both topic and genre, to self-select texts, to create their own post-reading activities, and to share their reading with other students and their teachers. The benefits of extensive reading include a pronounced development in language learning, including spelling, vocabulary, grammar, and text structure; increased knowledge of world; improved reading rates; improved writing skills, greater intrinsic motivation and enjoyment of reading, a more positive attitude toward language learning, and a greater possibility of developing a life-long reading habit. However, many readers fail to **actively** pay attention to and study new vocabulary as they read. **Explicit** instruction of lexicon in the form of a student vocabulary log can help students expand, recall and use more lexicons in their speech and writing.

Vocabulary Log

1. Word: Emphasize (*v.*)
2. Definition in your own words: to make something sound more important
3. Synonyms: stress, highlight, accentuate, draw attention to, intensify
4. Parts of speech: emphatic (*adj.*), emphasis (*n.*), emphasized (past tense), emphasizing (part.)
5. Sentence: To emphasize the cognitive internalization of new vocabulary through repeated practice and connectivity, the workshop leader wrote this sentence.

As students read, teachers can also point out common phrases, words, or sentence structures that students can use when they write or speak. Only through repeated practice, including use of synonyms of related parts of speech, can students truly acquire new lexicon in the long-run.

The goal of vocabulary instruction should be to increase of students' **automaticity** in reading. L2 word recognition is much slower, less automatic, than L1 word recognition due to the amount of orthographic processing. Teaching students to read phonetically, to read faster, and to recognize partial words or words with letters missing can help to build their **automaticity**. TEFL teachers will often diagnose which of the 3,000 most common words students need to learn and develop materials (e. g., vocab lists, flash cards, vocab logs, semantic maps, contextual clue guessing, etc.) to better enhance students acquisition of the lexicon. It's important to remember that L2 learners often struggle to use various word forms (e. g., emphasis v. emphasize v. emphatic) and that vocabulary can easily be incorporated into **CLT**. For example, rather than instructing students to discuss their dream vacation in small groups, the teacher may provide a list of new words to include in their discussion (e.g., luxury, necessities, luggage, guidebook, etc.). The more opportunities given for independent development of English lexicon, the more likely students are to advance their understanding and production of vocabulary.

Words to Avoid

As students become more advanced in their use of English, you will notice a dramatic increase in their fluency and accuracy. However, many students struggle to advance the complexity of their ideas and lexical expressions at a similar rate. The college students I currently teach overuse words like : *make, bring, take, look, give, come, get, go, be, keep, do, say, good, interesting, people, we, it, they, this, thing, stuff,* and phrasal verbs *(e.g., bring on, come up with, get rid of)*, which too often makes their ideas appear overly simplistic to an advanced reader. Although these words are common in English speech, they are less common in intermediate- to advanced-level academic texts. L2 students are often not aware of the varying **registers** used in English. Language and lexicon change in accordance with audience and setting. For example, I speak differently to my boss than I do to my friends from high school. I use a more formal **register** with more academic lexicon with my boss and an informal **register** with more slang with my friends. It's important that advanced L2 learners be made aware of the different registers in English and certain words, such as those above, that would be considered of lower register or simplistic.

When correcting students' vocabulary, the goal should be to increase automaticity without dwelling too much on accuracy. When I read students' paper, I will highlight a couple words on each page (not 40 or 50) and simply ask them to provide synonyms or other expressions they could use to convey a more exact meaning. Students can refer to their vocabulary use to provide additional expressions.

Chapter 11 Reading and Vocabulary

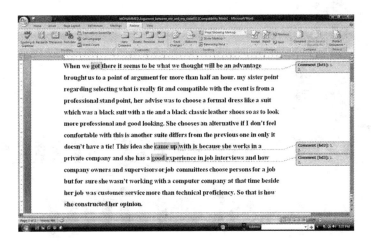

Guessing from Context

Good readers are often times good decoders and are able to interpret the text as it stands. **Decoding** means deriving meaning solely from the text. Through the use of automatic recognition and reading strategies, many new vocabulary words can be processed bottom-up: starting with a phonetic reading of the word, followed by a morphologic analysis, next looking at the surrounding lexicon and organizational patterns of the sentence, and finally drawing upon the theme or schemata of the text. Most students that are good decoders use bottom-up processing. Can you use your decoding skills to make sense of the messages below?

> John: I was mid star wars life saber app battle when conx was lost.
> Nancy: Nearly got in acc today, wheel came off on 90 going 60. Luckily I remembered what Mr. G said.
> Sign in China: Environmental sanitation of the scenic spot needs your conserve.
> French?: Cheri est ce que tu me comprends je t'aime j'envie de te voir a mes cote pour t'embrasser sans cesse.I NEED YOU DARLING bonne nuit LOVE.

Reflection and Activity for Teachers

1. With your group find one TEFL textbook to analyze. What is the target vocabulary? How was it chosen? Is the vocabulary taught incidentally or explicitly? How important does vocabulary seem to the textbook? Are they single words or chunks? Are there opportunities for guessing? Please rate and discussion how successfully vocabulary is taught by this textbook.
2. Design a lesson that would increase your students' reading rates. Discuss your lesson with your group.

Speaking and Listening

Chapter 12

> The goals for this chapter are:
> ➢ To understand the teacher's role in an effective communicative language classroom.
> ➢ To understand the difference between locutionary, ilocutionary, and perlocutionary acts.
> ➢ To create effective speaking and listening TEFL activities.

We often equate being able to speak a language with knowing the language. As Nunan (1991) writes, "Success is measured in terms of the ability to carry out a conversation in the target language." In the same way that notes on a piece of sheet music are not the actual music, words on a page, from the perspective of speech, are not the real language. If the goal of your TEFL class is to enable your students to communicate in English (and 99% of your teaching in Shenzhen will focus on this goal), the practicing speaking and listening skills should predominate your syllabus.

Native or Near-Native Speaker Credibility

You may not realize it, but you are a specialist with regard to the English language. Being a native or near-native speaker of English, your ability to correctly pronounce words, phrases, and sentences goes without saying. You represent a rare opportunity for your classes to learn English from a live and credible model. For many of your students, you may be the first native or near-native speaker of English that they've ever met and a representative of your country and culture—a responsibility which you should never underestimate. Although you may feel nervous as a new teacher, it's important to remember that your students want to like you. Likewise, they want to feel confident that they are going to learn English from a credible instructor, a feat that may have often eluded them in the past. So don't hesitate to be yourself and act like you know what you're doing!

Teacher Talk

A key rule to TEFL instruction is to limit the amount of time the teacher talks. Your English is likely fine; you're your students who need more time and practice speaking English. Think about how you can make your instructions clear and brief. Speak slowly and grade your language appropriately. Rather than repeat directions to activities, call on individual students to repeat them to you. Never ask, "Does everyone understand?" but rather ask your students to demonstrate understanding verbally. When students have finished an activity, don't forget to check for understanding. In China, whose culture may be face-conscious than yours, students may mask the fact that they haven't understood the teacher by smiling, giggling, or nodding rather than embarrassing themselves before their peers. The most effective way experienced TEFL teachers limit their teacher talk is to show rather than tell, meaning they model how to perform the activity as if they were students rather than directing as a teacher.

Modeling is key to effective TEFL instruction. Some of the activities may be new to the students. They may not catch on to how to do them just from oral instructions. Therefore, you need to reinforce your oral instructions with written instructions on the board or physical modeling. For example, if assigning a pair activity, call one of your better students and act out the activity with that student. For something complicated, you can rehearse with a student beforehand. If it's an individual activity, act it out yourself. If, for example, you're asking students to plot a Venn diagram, do one on the board first.

Recycle Activities

There are several reasons for recycling good activities. First, the class enjoyed them the first time and will look forward to participating in them again more often than not. Second, the class will already be familiar with the rules, and so less time will be spent on teacher talk. Third, most people forget 85% of what they read within 24 hours. This estimate has relevance for language learning. Teaching should devote time and energy to reviewing and practicing grammar and vocabulary from previous lessons. Time spent on review is never time wasted. Furthermore, recycling activities can save you time and energy creating new activities and materials every week. Finally, recycled activities emphasize the focus should be on language learning rather than the teacher's creativity to devise new and entertaining games to grab students' attention each and every day.

You can also recycle conversations. Part of speaking fluently is speaking faster. You may notice that your students' speech is filled with long pauses, stammers, and stops and starts. This is largely because they are thinking in their L1 and then translating into English. You want to get students out of this habit. A good way to do this to create a double ring in the classroom (you may need to find other ways in large classes):

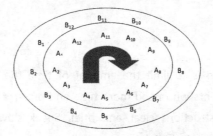

Partner A is allotted five minutes to tell a story to Partner B. If Partner A pauses or begins to repeat herself, then and only then, can Partner B interrupt and ask a follow-up question. After five minutes, Partner B takes her turn. Once both partners have practiced telling their story, the inner ring move one spot in a clockwise direction. In other words, A_1 now faces B_{12} and A_2 now faces B_1. The new pairs must repeat their same story, but are now only allotted four minutes. Once both partners have finished, the inner ring moves one more spot and are allotted three minutes, and on and on. In this way, students have multiple chances to practice speaking with greater speed and accuracy. The teacher can stand in the center of the rings and alá the panopticon creating an illusion of simultaneously monitoring all students' participation.

Circulate

Circulate around the classroom and monitor groups and pairs involved in the activity. Make your presence felt! While walking around, keep your eyes focused on an area of the room not directly in front of you. When you stand in front of someone, of course he or she will be working; it's those on the other side of the room you need to worry about. Let your students feel that you are always a few steps away to provide individual assistance but that you are always monitoring the class as a whole. Sometimes, you can address the class from the back of the room instead of the front. This lets students in the back know that they can't hide. A simple way to discourage a student prone to poor classroom behavior is to stand quietly stand beside him or her. The majority of your students' eyes will naturally shift to where you are standing and the potentially disruptive behavior will placed under a spotlight.

Chapter 12 Speaking and Listening

Pragmatics

Conversations involve more than just the literal language spoken. The context behind what is said can be just as important if not more important than the words themselves. **Pragmatics** is a subfield of linguistics that seeks to determine how the manner, time, place, etc. of speech gives meaning to the somewhat ambiguous literal translation. J.L. Austin (1967) divides a speech act into three components: (1) locutionary acts (2) ilocutionary, and (3) perlocutionary acts. A **locutionary act** is the literal meaning of the utterance, including its phonetic, morphological, syntactical, and semantic aspects. An **ilocutionary** act, however, is the intent of the utterance. For example, if I'm driving in my friend's car and say, "It's cold in here," the ilocutionary force of this speech act is to attempt to get my friend to turn on the heater. The perlocutionary act is the consequence of what was said. For example, my friend turns on the heater. Commanding, requesting, persuading, scaring, motivating are examples of perlocutionary acts that attempt to get the listener to understand or do something. "Go to bed now!" is a command given by one in a position of authority to one in a position of subservience. The perlocutionary effect of this speech act would differ significantly in an interaction between a prison guard and a recalcitrant inmate versus an interaction between two college roommates. "I'm sorry to have eaten the last chocolate bon-bon," is an apology, the act of which seeks to mediate potential conflict or hurt feelings. But how do you know if the apology is sincere? One of the hardest aspects of learning a second language is to separate the ilocutionary and perlocutionary acts from the locutionary act.

Following are some sample activities which raise TEFL students' awareness of the pragmatics behind their speech.

Follow-Up Questions

I noticed that my Chinese students, even those who had studied English for 12 or more years, tended to give very short answers to questions and rarely asked questions to me or others in English. Here's a typical conversation between a teacher and her students:

■ **A BAD CONVERSATION**

A: How are you?   B: Fine.
A: What did you do last weekend?   B: Nothing.
A: How are your classes?   B: Okay.
A: Do you like movies?   B: Sometimes.
A: What's your favorite animal?   B: Horses.

■ A BETTER CONVERSATION

A: How are you?   B: Fine.
A: Hmm... fine. Not excellent? Why is anything bothering you?
B: No, not really. I just don't have much to say.

A：Yeah, I know what you mean; it's hard trying to start a conversation! Why do you think is that?

B：It takes a long time for me to feel comfortable with someone.

A：And do you feel comfortable now?　　B：A little, but I don't like being in class.

A：Me Neither! Nobody likes being in class, don't you think so?

B：Yeah, but I have to take this class... I want to learn how to speak in English!

A：Oh, cool. How long have you studied English? Why do you want to study English? Do you enjoy it? Why not another class?

Asking follow up questions (who, what, when, where, and why) is a pragmatic skill that students need to practice to extend conversations and increase fluency. Also, notice in the better conversation above the use of fillers (hmm, yeah, oh, etc.). You can teach your students to use fillers to avoid awkward pauses and to show and take greater interest in the other partners' speech. Also, repeating back what you hear ("Hmmm... fine.") is a pragmatic skill that can effectively empower students to become teachers themselves. I teach three pragmatic skills from the first day of class, and in classes of 50 or more students find it a necessity. Not only do students begin to use English in more **authentic** ways, they now begin to recognize context and interactions with different individuals can affect the meaning of a speech act. In this way, students teach themselves and other rather than passively waiting for the teacher to direct the conversation (i.e., student-centered vs. teacher-centered learning).

Once students understand the importance of asking follow-up questions, showing interest, and extending the conversation, your job as a TEFL instructor becomes much easier. Rather than writing lengthy dialogues, you can simply pair students and provide them short prompts such as those below:

A: What do you like to do for fun?　　A: What are your plans for this summer?

B: I like movies.　　B: Nothing.

A: How's everything?

B: So-so.

You can time students to see how many follow-up questions they can ask their partners within a given period of time.

Establishing Rapport

Teaching is not a one-way street. The quicker you develop rapport with your classes, the better. You can review the principles of individualization and personalization for some ideas on how to nurture rapport with your students. Make an effort to understand why your students want to learn English. Begin new courses by distributing a questionnaire to your class which elicits goals for English learning, favorite topics, or issues they prefer not to discuss in class. Discussing the results of the questionnaire with the class will help you as a teacher to understand more about your students, while reinforcing their intrinsic motivation to improve through self-reflection.

Chapter 12 Speaking and Listening

Many will be obsessed with English as a means of earning a good grade on a national exam. However, you can constantly remind them of other reasons (practical, cultural, professional opportunities) that make it worthwhile to study English, including more opportunities to speak with you!

Here's a great way to begin a new class. Ask students to place the following items in the Venn diagram according to responsibility.

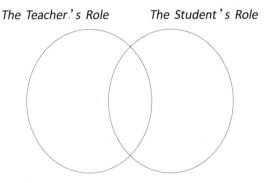

The Teacher's Role   The Student's Role

A. Evaluating work
B. Treating others with respect
C. Keeping a record of materials covered
D. Listening to others
E. Tutoring
F. Deciding students' learning objectives
G. Being punctual
H. Helping others
I. Attending class regularly
J. Being prepared for class
K. Reviewing material when absent
L. Sharing ideas
M. Contributing to discussions
N. Talking about their culture
O. Preparing course content
P. Explaining grammar
Q. Speaking clearly
R. Answering questions
S. Providing variety of activities
T. Being sure everyone speaks

Request, Commands, and Apologies

One big difference between Chinese and English is the use of honorifics. **Honorifics** are words used to convey respect or formality toward an elder, superior, or authority figure. In Chinese, *Ni hao*! is used for informal greetings while *Nin hao*! is used to display greater honor toward the recipient. Many Chinese students are unaware that English also contains various registers for expressing formality or informality. *Sir* or *ma'am* is obviously more formal than *boy* or *girl*. *What's up?* is considered more informal than *How are you?* While *You must help me!* shows less respect for the recipient than *Would you minding helping me, please?* Raising your students' level of awareness of the pragmatic considerations involved in their speech acts can go a long way toward avoiding negative social encounters with English speakers.

For example, people apologize in different ways. If someone complains about the noise from your stereo, you can:

Apologize and ... admit a mistake   "I'm sorry. I didn't realize it was so loud."
                     give an excuse   "Forgive me, I forgot I left it on."

make an offer "I'll turn it down, if you turn down your TV."
make a promise "Sorry, but this is my favorite song. I promise to turn it down in a minute."

Commands	Requests
Show me your homework!	Can you show me your homework?
You must turn down the stereo!	Would you turn down the stereo, please?
You have to drive me to school!	Would mind driving me to school?

Place students in groups of 4 or 5 and have them take turns asking and answering various requests (e.g., Could you lend me twenty dollars? Can you help me move into my new apartment tomorrow? Would you mind not smoking here?). If students answer no, they should provide a polite excuse (e.g., I'm sorry I can't lend you twenty dollars, I left my wallet at home.). After a few minutes, instruct student to role play different characters (e.g., a police officer, a grandmother, a young child, etc.). Students should begin to recognize how pragmatic changes in context affect the language used.

Changing the Topic

With more advanced classes a fun pragmatic skill to practice is how to change the topic from something boring to something of greater interest. In the following conversation, Bob is a car enthusiast and rambles on and on about his favorite car. Julie, however, is bored by car talk and wants to change the conversation to requesting Bob's help in babysitting her children.

A Bad Example:

Bob: Man, did you see that car? That was a Lotus EXL 420 Turbo with jet fuel injection, 900 horsepower engine ... it can go from 0 to 120kmh in about 4 seconds. The only faster car on Earth is a Ferrari GTO ...

Julie: Yeah, whatever. You want to take care of our children tonight?

Bob: What? No.

You can teach students how to improve their conversation skills and keep the discussion flowing without awkward shifts in direction by following four simple steps. (1) Listen to your partner and show interest; (2) Ask a follow-up question; (3) Find a connection between the two topics; and (4) Slowly but explicitly introduce the new topic.

A Good Example:

Bob: Man, did you see that car? That was a Lotus EXL 420 Turbo with jet fuel injection, 900 horsepower engine ... it can go from 0 to 120kmh in about 4 seconds. The only faster car on Earth is a Ferrari GTO ...

Julie: A Ferrari GTO? Yeah, too bad they cost $400,000. You'll never be able to afford that!

Bob: But did you see how beautiful it looks! If I had that car I'd always be out driving around, showing it off to everyone!

Julie: That's only if you didn't have kids and responsibilities. Speaking of which, I'd like to go out tonight and eat dinner with some friends. Would you mind babysitting the children? I'll pay you, and you can start saving up for your dream car.

Bob: Ha ha. Yeah, sure no problem. What time do you want me?

Once students have understood the model, you can place them into groups of four and five and give them a topic to discuss. After a few minutes and once the conversations get flowing, the teacher can secretly hand a notecard with a new topic written on it (e.g., shopping, pets, cars, weather, etc.) to one member of the group. That member must then attempt to change the topic of conversation in a smooth and natural manner. This activity is easy to prepare and can last for a long time in high-intermediate to advanced classes. While it appears to be an open-ended activity, the targeted skill of changing topics provides structure and enhances students' learning. Changing the topic, awareness of honorifics, and asking follow-up questions are examples of activities that introduce learners to the pragmatic functions of English speaking and listening.

Reflection and Activity for Teachers

1. With your group make a list of other pragmatic functions of English speaking and listening other than the ones included above.
2. Devise an activity for two of the functions your group has listed to raise your students' awareness of that particular pragmatic function of English speaking and listening.

Listening

The explicit instruction of listening in the TEFL classroom first became popular in the 1960s with the **audio-lingual method** (**ALM**). **ALM** simply put is teacher says, students repeat.

T: Good morning, students.	S: Good morning, teacher.
T: How are you today?	S: How are you today?
T: I'm great!	S: I'm great!
T: Do you like pizza?	S: Do you like pizza?
T: Yes, I do!	S: Yes, I do!

ALM is a very simple approach to teaching, and Chinese students, especially younger ones, may enjoy these teacher-directed approaches as opposed to more student-centered activities. Unfortunately, less than a decade after ALM was first introduced, a surfeit of research indicated that students largely failed to acquire the targeted language and retain the lesson.

Berlitz Method

The **Berlitz** or **direct method** of language learning was introduced in the late 19th century by Maximillan Berlitz and has grown to become the most popular mode of private language instruction in the world. The Berlitz method follows ALM in that grammar is taught inductively and all instruction is done in the target language (L2). There is no emphasis on reading and writing, which is why the Berlitz Method is recommended for business travelers, but not necessarily for students wanting to achieve accuracy, fluency, and complexity in an L2. Here's an example script in Spanish following the direct method. (If you already know basic Spanish, think how you would teach the same lesson in another language.)

 T: (points to book) Libro.
 S: (points to book) Libro.
 T: Bien! (points to pen) Pluma.
 S: Pluma.
 T: Perfecto. (points to book) Esto es un libro.
 S: (points to book) Esto es un libro.
 T: (points to pen) Esto es una pluma.
 S: Esto es una pluma.
 T: Si o no. (points to book) Esto es un libro?
 S: (looks confused)
 T: Si, (nods head) esto es un libro.
 S: Ah, si, esto es un libro.
 T: (points to pen). Si or no, esto es un libro?
 S: No, esto es libro.
 T: No, (points to book) esto no es un libro. Esto es una pluma. Repita por favor.
 S: Este no es un libro. Este es un pluma.
 T: Bien! (points to book) Este es una pluma?
 S: No, este no es una pluma. Este es un libro.
 T: Ahora, preguntame (motions toward herself).
 S: (points to book) Este ... es ... un... libro?
 T: Si, este es un libro.
 S: (points to pen) Este ... es un libro?
 T: No, este es un libro. Este es una pluma.

Two Strategies to Listening

Similar to reading, students employ two simultaneous strategies when listening: bottom-up and top-down. The **bottom-up** strategy refers listening to the smallest parts of speech (phonemes) to decode morphemes, then decoding individual words, and finally decoding sentences. In so doing, the listener acts like a tape recorder and attempts to distinguish and record even the smallest units of language spoken. The **top-down** strategy refers to how the listener constructs meaning based on the sound clues. The listener may use background knowledge of the topic being spoken and rely on context, situation, and previous lessons to guess the larger meaning of the speech act. It's important to recognize that both strategies are necessary for successful listening in an L2.

How to Build an Effective Listening Activity

The first step of building an effective listening activity is to choose authentic listening materials. Given the ubiquity of internet videos, textbook cassettes, TV news programs, movies, TV shows, radio broadcasts, podcasts, etc., it shouldn't be too hard to find an authentic recording. Remember, however, the selected recording should challenge your students without overwhelming them ($i + 1$) and draw from their interests rather than yours.

Once you have found an authentic recording, the second step is to create a **pre-listening** activity. Research shows that **schema building** tasks (see Reading & Writing chapter 11) before listening will reinforce the acquisition of new vocabulary, meaning, and context. Common pre-listening activities may include:

- Multiple choice/guessing the meaning of new vocabulary;
- Brainstorming on the topic;
- Predicting what words or ideas will be presented in the recording;
- Debating or discussing the topic as a class or in small groups;
- Writing questions they have about the topic and attempting to answer them with a partner;
- Background or history needed to contextualize the recording (e.g., Before students listen to a news story on Michael Jackson's funeral, the teacher presents a brief of Michael Jackson's life).

Now, students are ready to listen. But there's a difference between passive and **active listening**. In the next step, as students listen to the recording, the teacher should provide them with the structure of what to listen for. One common way of accomplishing this task is to provide students with **preset questions** that can only be answered by understanding or decoding the recording. A second common way is to teach students note-taking skills, such as the Cornell Method, that require students to outline main ideas while replicating key words and quotations (i.e. bottom-up and top-down processing). Whatever approach you choose, it's also important to consider the different skills required for **extensive** listening—one long recording or several short recording designed to focus students' listening on big-picture idea or summarization of main ideas—or **intensive** listening—a shorter recording designed to focus students' listening to sentence-, word-, or smaller-level aspects of the recording. Based on the length, speed, and difficulty of the recording and your students' *i*-level you may need to replay the recording a second or third time.

Finally, no listening activity should be complete without some form of a **post-listening** activity. A post-listening activity requires students to recall the information or material from the recording. Common post-listening activities may include:

- Students check answers to preset questions and discuss with a partner;
- Using their notes students summarize or paraphrase the recording in their own words;
- Students compare notes for main ideas v. supporting ideas; essential v. non-essential information;
- Students role play the recording;
- Class debate or discussion of the ideas presented in the recording;
- Class examines the pragmatic aspects of the recording including conversational strategies and inferred meaning.

Sample Speaking and Listening Activities

Following are some tried and tested examples of speaking and listening activities commonly employed in the TEFL classroom. Read through each activity and consider how you would adapt and/or revise the lesson for your students. Remember no sample lesson plan will work uniformly for all classes, as students are individuals and not borg units.

Discrimination Exercises

Listen to the teacher. Circle the word you hear.

- A. fourteen   forty
- B. fifteen   fifty
- C. sixteen   sixty
- D. thirteen   thirty
- E. seventeen   seventy

Dictations

- Read at a fairly normal speed.
- Read each phrase 3 times.
- Read all the way through the last time.
- Score for comprehension, not spelling, etc.
- Put passage up on overhead for Ss to score their own.

Chapter 12 Speaking and Listening

Bingo Games

- Have students draw a grid with 16-25 squares.
- Give them a list of vocabulary words- more words than they have squares (use words they have trouble distinguishing).
- They write the words in the boxes on their squares in whatever order they want.
- Draw the words randomly and call them out. Students mark the words on their bingo cards with markers, squares of paper or Xs.
- First student to get boxes in a straight line, up and down, across or corner to corner wins.

Picture Boxes

- Have students draw grid on paper— 9 to 16 squares.
- Give instructions—"Draw an apple in the top right corner." Use vocabulary you've been studying.
- Draw them yourself on a transparency as you give the instructions or have one prepared ahead.
- Put transparency up for students to check their grids.

Instructions

Give instructions for a task. For example:
- Fold a piece of paper in half lengthwise.
- Fold one corner back to the middle.
- Fold the other corner on the same end back to the middle.
- Fold one side back to the middle.
- Fold the other side back to the middle.
- What do you have?

Tapes and Videos

- Prepare students with key vocabulary before playing.
- Play video with sound off first- discuss what Ss saw.
- Play short segments- beginning learners can only follow very short segments.
- Play several times with questions in between to focus attention.
- Ask global questions first, more specific questions as Ss comprehend more of the language.

Speaking Activities

Your primary goal as a TEFL in China instructor will likely be to build students' spoken fluency. The more opportunities your students have to speak, the better! Experienced TEFL instructors keep a folder of successful activities, share their ideas with other instructors, borrow from them and other websites, books, and sources, and constantly attempt to revise and improve their teaching. Common speaking activities in the TEFL classroom include: games, stories from pictures, dialogues, role playing, improvisations, simulations, plays, interviews, mock-radio/TV broadcasts, impromptu speeches, and debates. The more variety you include in the speaking classroom the better. Keep students guessing and they'll be more likely to get interested and to speak!

Visual Fluency

There's a saying that a picture is worth thousand words. Visuals are extremely effective in the TEFL classroom and are used quite often to assess students' fluency, accuracy, and complexity of speech.

Design Your Dream Home

Student A describes her dream home/favorite room to Student B. Student B draws a picture or blueprint of the dream home, keeping the picture hidden from Student A. After 5-10 minutes, the roles switch and Student B describes her dream home/favorite room. When both partners have finished, the students compare their pictures and discuss the acuity of their listening skills. This works especially for the teaching of preposition, rooms, and furniture-related vocabulary (e.g. There's a swimming pool on top of the house next to my music studio.).

Describe the Picture

When I taught in China, I brought pictures of my family, friends, and home with me. My students loved seeing me at different stages of my life ("What happened to you, laoshi, you used to be skinny?") and getting to see glimpses of American culture. Divide the class into two and show the right half of the room Picture A (five seconds) while the left half closes their eyes and Picture B (five seconds) while the right half closes their eyes. The right half must then find a partner from the left and describe their picture in as much detail as possible while the partner attempt to draw on a separate sheet of paper. As the activity dies down, the teacher can put both pictures back on the screen and ask students to compare and contrast.

Chapter 12 Speaking and Listening

  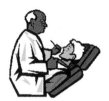

Tell me what's happening in this picture.

Chain Stories: Cinderella

Your students likely are familiar with some popular American cartoons or fairy tales, but you may want to ask them before preparing a lesson like the one below. Students are placed into groups of 4-5 and are given a series of pictures to prompt them into creating a story. The story can be the same as the original or students can go off script and create alternative versions. Remember the focus is on fluency, getting students to speak in English as much as possible, rather than on creating an Academy Award-winning story. The first student begins the story, "Once upon a time..." and speaks for one minute, then the second continues the story, and on and on until the class' interest begins to die down.

If your high school students find this activity to be silly or easy, you can always adapt or revise it with discussion questions like those below in place of or following the chain story.

1. Compare how your story differs from the original story.
2. Why do you think Cinderella has become such a popular story?
3. Analyze the gender roles portrayed in the story.
4. Do you think this story is suitable for young girls? Why/why not?
5. Could you make a better fairy tale to teach young girls an important moral lesson?

Pictionary/ Reverse Pictionary / Charades

The popular board game is also a time-tested standby to warm-up or end a class. Students are divided into teams and one student is chosen at random to draw a picture of a vocabulary word selected by the teacher. The first student to shout out (or, better yet, if there's another class going on next door, raise their hand) and correctly guess the vocabulary word gets one point. For reverse Pictionary, the teacher shows the chosen student a picture rather than a vocabulary word (e.g., a picture of an airplane). The student must then describe the picture to the class without saying the targeted vocabulary word (e.g., it's a vehicle with wings and a motor that flies through the air). The first group to correctly guess the word gets one point.

Movies and Videos

Most Chinese students love English-language movies, but be careful! Showing movies without targeting a particular skill or language focus can turn your class into a playhouse and demotivate students when you attempt to teach them in other ways. The use of movies in the TEFL classroom should be used sparingly as a reward and not as the sole method of instruction. Many movie and TV scripts can be downloaded for free from websites like: http://www.corky.net/scripts/ and http://www.eslnotes.com/. In little time, you can erase a few words from the script and ask to students to fill in the blanks as they listen to one selected scene. You can also invite students to read their script along with the actors' voice to practice their pronunciation. Movies are also a good way to introduce students to cultural issues, slang, and idioms that may not appear in their English textbooks. Better yet, you can always stop the movie and discuss or debate what was shown. In these ways, movies and video can be used to effectively teach speaking, listening, pronunciation, vocabulary, culture and more. Of course, it is highly recommended that you consider the age, interests, and level of your students before choosing your videos.

Structured Role Play

Ordering in a restaurant
A: Ask B what he wants to drink.
B: Say that you want some tea.
A: Ask B what he wants to eat.
B: Say that you want a salad and a hamburger.
A: Ask B what kind of salad dressing he wants.
B: Say that you want French dressing.

One Part Dialogues

A: _____?
B: I'd like a cup of coffee, please.
A: _____?
B: I'd like a salad and a hamburger.
A: _____?
B: I'd like French dressing.

Chapter 12 Speaking and Listening

Response to Situations

- You stepped on someone's toe and that person is in pain. What do you say?
- Someone you don't know very well invited you to a party, but you can't go. What do you say?
- A classmate asks to borrow your book tonight, but you want to use it. What do you say?

Reflection and Activity for Teachers

1. Which of the sample activities do you like most for your students? Why?
2. With a group create two more activities that combine listening and speaking to improve students' English fluency. Compare your activities with another group and discuss.

CTLC leader William O'Donnel and coordinator James meeting with Shenzhen Education Bureau leaders

Pronunciation

Chapter 13

The goals for this chapter are:
> To improve our understanding of the pronunciation of sounds, words, sentences, and longer speech patterns.
> To learn strategies for teaching pronunciation in the Chinese TEFL classroom.
> To build students' confidences in their English pronunciation abilities.

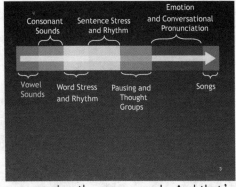

Reflection:

One thing that I overlooked in my first few years as an TEFL instructor was just how many dialects of English existed. From England to Australia to South Africa to India to the West Indies to Singapore to Newfoundland, I encountered native English speakers same soundswith different ways of pronouncing the same sounds. And that's not even mentioning the sub-dialects within particular countries: North v. South, urban v. rural, older generation v. younger generation, male v. female, rich vs. poor, and the various ethnic groups within each country. Who was I to correct someone's pronunciation to conform more closely to my own? What I quickly realized was that

Chapter 13 Pronunciation

the key to pronunciation was simply being understood. What's more, after several more years of TEFL teaching, I realized that my own ability to listen and understand different accents could also improve. In other words, pronunciation is a two-way street; TEFL teachers need to improve their pronunciation listening as well.

One thing I love about travelling around China and speaking in Chinese is when those I meet inevitably tell me, "You speak Chinese so well! Your pronunciation is perfect!" Of course, I know this is not true as I struggle with the four tones and other different sounds that appear in Chinese but not in American English, but I still like to hear it. It's only natural that we don't enjoy our pronunciation to be criticized or overly corrected. Our way of enunciating is very personal— it's how we talk and who we are. Pronunciation is also very, very hard to change, especially after we've been moving our lips, tongue, and teeth in one manner for several decades. One big reason why Chinese students may appear shy and reluctant to speak English aloud is that they are afraid of being corrected or misunderstood. Therefore, it is essential as a TEFL instructor to: 1) offer encouragement when teaching pronunciation, 2) allow for individual differences in accents, and 3) listen actively for understanding rather than for conformity with your native accent.

Although we mainly consider pronunciation from a phoneme, or one single-sound, level. I've found it more productive to teach pronunciation on higher levels: syllables, words, sentences, and dialogues. In this chapter, we'll slowly build upon effective tools for TEFL pronunciation instruction!

PHONEMES

What are vowels?

$$\textbf{Vowels} \begin{cases} a, e, i, o, u, \\ \text{and sometimes y} \end{cases} \qquad \textbf{Consonants} \begin{cases} b, c, d, f \\ g, h, j, k \\ l, m, n, p \\ q, r, s, t \\ v, w, x, y, z \end{cases}$$

What is the difference between a vowel sound and a consonant sound?

When discussing pronunciation we distinguish between a letter and a single sound, aka a **phoneme**. Phonemes involve articulation—the movement of the lips, tongue, teeth, mouth, and vocal cords; letters are simply written representations of sounds (and can cause a great deal of difficulty in the case of English where one letter does not always equate to only one sound). Phonemes are differentiated from letters like this: /s/, /æ/ or /θ/. All of the phonetic symbols from the world's languages comprise an alphabet known as the IPA or International Phonetic Alphabet. Most Chinese students are familiar with the IPA and have been taught the IPA from an early age in their language instruction. We will use IPA throughout this chapter and you should familiarize yourself with the IPA symbols. For the most part, English and Chinese are comprised of the same phonemes although there are a few differences. For example, Chinese lacks the /θ/ or "th" sound, English lacks the four tones.

Consonants are produced by contact between the lips, teeth, tongue and mouth palate.

Vowels have no touching.

That's why it's important to open your mouth

W I D E

when practicing vowel sounds.

Front Vowel Sounds

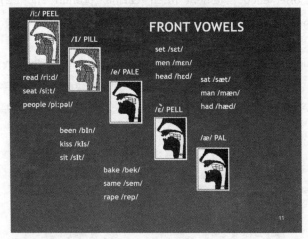

There are five front vowel phonemes in English. For each, it's important to keep the mouth open wide and the tongue positioned in the front of the mouth. The tongue moves from the top palate /i:/ to just below the top row of teeth /I/ to the middle of the mouth /e/ to just above the lower row of teeth /ɛ/ to the bottom palate /æ/.

My favorite way to teach these vowel sounds is through a little TPR. If I say Peel, students touch their heads. If I say Pill, students touch their shoulders. Pale = stomach; Pell = knees; Pal = feet. After several practices as a class, I break students into small groups and have them play the game among themselves. This is a popular warm-up activity that can be used to start nearly any ESOL class.

Back Vowel Sounds

There are four back vowel phonemes in American English and five in British English. For each, it's again important to keep the mouth open wide but the tongue is now positioned in the back of the mouth. The tongue moves from the top palate /u:/ to just below the top row of teeth /U/

Chapter 13 Pronunciation

to the middle of the mouth /o/ to just above the lower row of teeth / ɔ/ to the very bottom palate /ɑ/.

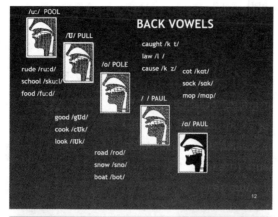

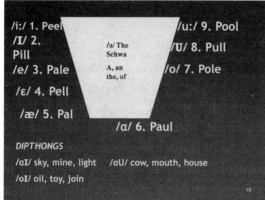

A visual diagram like the one above can help students visualize the position of the tongue in the mouth for each vowel sound. I will say one of the words (e.g., Pole) and ask students to hold up the number of fingers beside the word (e.g., 7). After several practices as a class, students break up into small groups and practice these sounds among themselves.

Diphthongs are defined as two combined vowel phonemes. Say /a/ with your tongue at the very bottom back of your mouth. Now move say /I/ moving your tongue to the front of your mouth just below the teeth. Try again, but a little faster, then faster, then faster. Eventually you should hear the diphthong /aI/ as in "rice." Diphthongs do not appear in Chinese, so your student may need additional time to practice these sounds.

IPA will help your students to read any new word and pronounce it correctly. By teaching reading phonetically, you can ensure your students will have a lifetime of independent reading and language learning.

Notice /i:/, /e/, /u:/, and /o/ most often contains two vowels next to each other. For example, read, main, food, and boat. The other vowel sounds usually have only one vowel between two consonants. For example, hit, ten, fat, hop, etc. Putting an "e" at the end of the word will make the vowel longer. For example, compare "car" vs. "care"; "pet" vs. "Pete"; "kit" vs. "kite"; "dud" vs. "dude" * Although these rules commonly apply, there are many,

many exceptions to these rules. Be careful!!

If you learned how to read phonetically, you should have no difficulty pronouncing these made-up words correctly and teach

doit /doIt/	sote /sot/	mabe /meb/
clar /klær/	foy /foI/	vun /vUn/
fim /fIm/	dright /draIt/	jern /dʒɛrn/
moof /muf/	spoud /spaUd/	hupe /hup/
yot /yɑt/	rud /rUd/	heest /hi:st/
sny /snaI/	mog /mag/	hep /hɛp/
stook /stu:k/	glay /gle/	flirch /flIrtʃ/
shain /ʃen/	porth /pUrθ/	sib /sIb/
weam /wi:m/	lurst /lUrst/	cag /kæg/
foap /fop/		

Reflection:

When I was teaching in Longgang, China, my vice-principle asked me whether I'd be willing to give a pronunciation workshop to the English teachers in my school. It seems that even these highly trained and highly experienced professionals were anxious about their English pronunciation. Luckily, I had been trained in the TEFL program and knew it would be fairly easy to put together some tongue twisters and minimal pairs. (I didn't know at the time there were other, more effective ways to teach pronunciation.) I led two one-hour pronunciation workshops and was thanked by my grateful vice-principle and colleagues. Later, when I asked for the number of my office hours per week to be reduced, the consent was nearly immediate. The old "scratch my back, and I'll scratch yours" logic was put into effect. In other words, teaching pronunciation is universally appreciated, relatively easy, and can be a great bargaining chip!

Sing a Song

♪ **I Like to Eat Apples and Bananas**
I like to eat eat eat apples and bananas.
I like to eat eat eat apples and bananas.
/i:/ I like to eat eat eat eaples and beeneenees.
/I/ I like to it it it ipples and bininis.
/e/ I like to ate ate ate aiples and baynaynays.
/ɛ/ I like to et et et epples and benenes.
/æ/ I like to at at at apples and bananas.
/u:/ I like to ute ute ute ooples and boonoonoos.
/U/ I like to ut ut ut upples and bununus.

/o/ I like to oat oat oat oaples and boenoenoes.
/ɑ/ I like to ot ot ot opples and bononos.
/aI/ I like to ite ite ite iples and bienienies.
/oI/ I like to oyt oyt oyt oyples and boynoynoys.

Continuant vs. Stop

One way to differentiate the articulation of consonant phonemes is via the flow of air through the mouth. **Continuants** are phonemes in which air streams continuously through the lips as in /s/, /f/, or /r/.

If the air flow is stopped and let out in a single rush of air as in /b/, /t/, or /g/, the phoneme is classed as a **stop**. Hold your hand next to your mouth and practice the following sounds. Which are stops and which are continuants?

/f/ vs. /p/		/v/ vs. /b/		/dʒ/ vs. /z/	
1	2	1	2	1	2
fat	pat	vote	boat	Jane	Zane
fail	pail	very	berry	rage	raise
fine	pine	curve	curb	jest	zest
fool	pool	calves	cabs	age	"A's"

Voiced vs. Unvoiced

Another way to differentiate the articulation of consonant phonemes is via the Vibration of the vocal cords. Place your hand on your throat and say a continuous /z/. You should feel the vibration. /z/ is a **voiced** sound.

Unvoiced sounds are those in which the vocal cords do not vibrate. Place your hand on your throat and say a continuous /s/. You should not feel any vibration. Place your hand on your throat and practice the following sounds.

Which are voiced and which are unvoiced?

/b/ vs. /p/		/v/ vs. /f/		/θ/ vs. /ð/	
1	2	1	2	1	2

big	pig	van	fan	thigh	thy
cub	cup	vine	fine	teeth	teethe
by	pie	leave	leaf	bath	bathe
mob	mop	have	half	ether	either

Minimal Pairs

Minimal pairs are pairs of words that differ by only one phoneme. For example: "bet" and "bed." Using these pairs is a common tactic to help students recognize the minor differences in articulation. Keep in mind that students' pronunciation can improve not only by practicing speaking these minimal pairs but by listening and correctly identifying the minimal pair. In my classroom, I will read one of the following minimal pairs and ask students to hold up one or two fingers. Following this listening exercise, I ask students to practice in pairs or small groups.

/f/ vs. /p/		/v/ vs. /b/		/b/ vs. /p/		/v/ vs. /f/	
1	2	1	2	1	2	1	2
fat	pat	vote	boat	big	pig	van	fan
fail	pail	very	berry	cub	cup	vine	fine
fine	pine	curve	curb	by	pie	leave	leaf
fool	pool	calves	cabs	mob	mop	have	half

/dʒ/ vs. /z/		/θ/ vs. /ð/		/f/ vs. /θ/		/t/ vs. /θ/	
1	2	1	2	1	2	1	2
Jane	Zane	thigh	thy	fin	thin	tin	thin
Rage	raise	teeth	teethe	free	three	true	threw
Jest	zest	bath	bathe	fought	thought	tank	thank
Age	"A's"	ether	either	deaf	death	taught	thought

/θ/ vs. /z/		/θ/ vs. /s/		/s/ vs. /ʃ/		/s/ vs. /z/	
1	2	1	2	1	2	1	2
then	Zen	thin	sin	same	shame	bus	buzz
thee	'z'	thought	sought	sign	shine	hiss	his
clothe	close	thank	sank	seat	sheet	sue	zoo
clothing	closing	math	mass	sell	shell	rice	rise

/θ/ vs. /d/		/tʃ/ vs. /dʒ/		/tʃ/ vs. /ʃ/		/r/ vs. /l/	
1	2	1	2	1	2	1	2
they	day	chin	gin	chew	shoe	ray	lay
those	doze	choke	joke	watch	wash	row	low
Keith	keyed	chain	Jane	chop	shop	reap	leap
then	den	etch	edge	witch	wish	red	led

Chapter 13 Pronunciation

Telephone Codes

There are several games you can play with minimal pairs. Here's a simple example. The instructor tells the class a telephone number using one of the minimal pairs as codes. Students have to listen and write the number next to word they hear.

1. *pat*
2. *fat*
3. *moon*
4. *noon*
5. *leaf*
6. *leap*
7. *peel*
8. *pill*
9. *rake*
0. *lake*

For example, the teacher says "Pat, noon, leap, pill, rake."
And the students write 1-4-6-8-9.

Tongue Twisters

Everyone knows a few tongue twisters which help to focus on the pronunciation of individual or combined phonemes. Yes, they make us laugh, but they can also be an effective warm-up and teaching tool. I like to start slowly, reading one word at a time and having the students repeat after me. Then, I ask them to read the tongue twister faster and finally three times in a row. Here are some of my favorites:

1. Betty Bopper bought a bit of bitter butter to make her batter better, but the bitter butter she bought was too bitter.
2. A proper copper coffee pot.
3. Valuable valley villas.
4. Long-legged ladies last longer.
5. Ruby ran in the rain wearing a red raincoat.
6. Please tell Frank to turn right at the red light.
7. Freshly fried fresh flesh.
8. Theodore thought of three thousand, three hundred and thirty-three things on Thursday.
9. We surely shall see the sun shine soon.
10. She sells seashells by the sea shore, but the shells she sells are not seashells.
11. I slit the sheet, the sheet I slit, and on the slitted sheet I sit.
12. Peter Piper picked a peck of pickled peppers, how many peck of pickled peppers did Peter Piper pick?
13. Three free throws.
14. How much wood would a woodchuck chuck if a woodchuck could chuck wood?
15. Which wicked witch wished which wicked wish?
16. Chop shops stock chops.
17. While we were walking, we were watching window washers wash Washington's windows

with warm washing water.
18. Fred fed Ted bread, and Ted fed Fred bread.
19. The sixth sick sheik's sixth sheep's sick.

Syllabication

Across
How many vowels are there? _____
How many vowel sounds are there? _____
How many syllables are there? _____

Cheese
How many vowels are there? _____
How many vowel sounds are there? _____
How many syllables are there? _____

Beautiful
How many vowels are there? _____
How many vowel sounds are there? _____
How many syllables are there? _____

Counting Syllables

Read the following words with a partner and decide the number of syllables.

against _____   empty _____   battle _____
three _____   delicious _____ quietly _____
orange _____   dance _____   restaurant _____
costume _____   temple _____   wonderfully _____
dolphin _____   film _____   quarter _____
newspaper _____ koala _____   large _____

Past Tense "-ed"

Listen to the following words. Hold up one hand if you hear one syllable, and two hands if you hear two syllables.

planted   landed   worked   caused   planned   laughed
added   folded   treated   counted   hated   divided

Sometimes "-ed" is pronounced as an extra syllable; other times it is not. Can you explain the rule?

> **Reflection:**
> I've found that all too often we consider pronunciation from only a phoneme level. Getting students to change the way they've moved their lips, tongues, and teeth throughout most of their lives can be a nearly impossible task. For this reason, I've found it more productive to teach pronunciation on higher levels: syllables, words, sentences, and dialogues. Now, we'll slowly build toward these more effective tools for TEFL pronunciation instruction—tools which will help your students be understood!

The Schwa

Look at the following words:

forget   allow   arrive

What is the vowel sound of the first syllable?

___

Answer: the schwa sound /ə/. The schwa sound is not a true vowel sound, yet it is the most common vowel sound in the English language. /ə/ can only be explained as an unstressed vowel. Let your mouth and tongue go lax. Then, imagine a boxer hitting you in the stomach... "Uh!" That's the schwa sound; it's easy and comes out naturally without any stress.

Example: Banana = /bənænə/

Buh na nuh

Listening Practice: Identifying Schwa

Listen to these words. Draw a slash through the unclear vowels (schwa). Then practice saying the words.

1 clear vowel	2 clear vowels
problem	mathematics
printed	economics
drama	photography
needle	economy
computer	absolute
employment	application
requirement	international

Word Rhythm / Sentence Rhythm

Generally, Chinese students pick up quickly on word syllabication. What they often fail to realize is that sentences also have a rhythm similar to words. By connecting word rhythm to sentence rhythm you can draw your students' awareness to the natural intonation of English communication.

Listen and draw dots under the following pairs to show the rhythm pattern. Then, practice with a partner. One partner will say the word with the proper rhythm and the other partner will read the sentence using the exact same rhythm.

1. attractive   It's active.
   . • .   . • .

2. absolute   Have some fruit.
   . . •   . . •

3. responsible   It's possible.
4. electrification   I need a vacation!
5. scientific   I'm terrific!
6. photography   It's hard for me.
7. economic   This is chronic.
8. institution   Fight pollution!
9. pronunciation   Let's tell the nation!

* This activity was adapted from *Pronunciation Games* by Mark Hancock, Cambridge University Press, 1996.

Chanting

Here's a chanting activity also adapted from *Pronunciation Games* by Mark Hancock, Cambridge University Press, 1996. The teacher says the word on the far left three (e.g. "Dar, dar, dar") and the students repeat the rhythm with the words on the right (e.g. "Fresh fried chips.") Once the syllabication and rhythm are understood, the teacher can mix up the pattern (e.g., "Dar, dooby, dipety") to which the students must reply with the exact same rhythm (e.g. Fresh fish and sausages). By practicing these patterns fast and slow as a class, the teacher can model how native English speakers intone with rhythm in their speech. After a few times, I have students practice in pairs or in small groups.

Dar	Fresh	fried	chips
Dooby	Lots of	fish and	pizza
Dipety	Plenty of	carrots and	sausages
Dar	New	black	boots
Dooby	Lovely	yellow	trousers
Dipety	Horrible	rose colored	sunglasses

Dar	One	cold	beer
Dooby	Half a	glass of	whiskey
Dipety	Give me a	bottle of	orange juice

Limericks

Read the limerick and underline the words that receive the most emphasis.

There once was a lady from Niger
Who went for a ride on a tiger.
They returned from the ride
With the lady inside
And a smile on the face of the tiger.

You should have underlined: lady, Niger, ride, tiger, returned, ride, lady, inside, smile, face, tiger. Read just those words again, loudly, slowly, and clearly. LADY, NIGER, RIDE, TIGER, RETURNED, RIDE, LADY, INSIDE, SMILE, FACE, TIGER. The general meaning of the poem should remain clear. We call these **content words** as opposed to **structure words** like "a," "for," "and," "with," etc. which aren't usually stressed because they do not contain content only grammatical structure. Similar to texting today or telegrams one hundred ago, we know how to intuitively remove structure words from our speech yet still maintain the original meaning.

Practice these other limericks with your partner. Underline the most import words. Try to practice speaking quickly through the structure words and slower through the content words! Vary your speed.

Some teachers are quick to suggest
That we study quite hard for a test.
It takes lots of thought
To learn what we're taught.
But I think I'd prefer just to rest.

A student was sent to Tacoma
Intending to earn a diploma.
He said, "With the rain
I don't want to remain.
I think I'd prefer Oklahoma."

Reflection:

The primary difficulty I have had understanding Chinese students' pronunciation is not at the phonemic level, but at the sentence level. Specifically, in their rhythm, pausing, intonation, and emotion. These, I believe, are truly the keys to your students being understood by native English listeners.

Structure Words

Think of examples of structure words and list them below.

Pronouns	Prepositions	Articles	"to be"	Conjunction	Auxiliary Verbs
He	in	a	is	and	can

Circle the content words in the following sentences. Then, mark the stressed syllables in each content word. Practice reading the sentences with a partner.

1. What did your mother say about your new earrings?
2. Did you go to the park with your family last Saturday?
3. University students should study every day in order to succeed in their classes.
4. Is it harder to speak a new language or to hear and understand it?
5. Where do you enjoy going for your summer vacation?
6. Thomas went to Rome for his vacation and said that he loved the old architecture.

10 Tips for Standard American English Pronunciation

1. Sentence Stress

Read the following sentence and emphasize the different words. You should notice how the meaning of the sentence changes radically as the sentence stress shifts.

    Students can't kill their teachers.
      CAN'T

2. Linking

One way American English speakers speak faster is through linking consonant phonemes at the end of a word to vowel phonemes at the beginning of the following word.

    This / is / an / excellent /example.
     sss sss nnn ttt

Go back to the limericks. Do you see any words that can be linked together? Try reading the entire limerick one more time a little faster by linking these words.

Chapter 13 Pronunciation

3. Contractions

Another way American English speakers communicate faster is through contractions. Although your Chinese students are likely familiar with reading contractions, they may not have practiced their proper pronunciation.

Where will you stay? I am going to stay with my brother, did not you know?

Where'll you stay? I'm going to stay with my brother, didn't you know?

4. Linking /j/

"y" is a semi-vowel sound. As such, it can also be linked to preceding consonant phonemes. The linkage however often produces a /ʤ/ sound.

Did you hear that? Would you tell it to me?

Didja Wouldja

5. Reduced /t/

When /t/ is surrounded by two vowel sounds, many American English speakers will reduce the phoneme to /d/. This drives British English speakers crazy!

The water? Oh yes! Please put it over there.

The wader? Oh yes! Please pudidover there.

6. Linking Vowels

When two vowel phonemes appear at the end of one word and the beginning of the next, American English speakers will often link them together through the addition of an extra /w/ or /j/ phoneme.

Doe a deer. Free ice. The end.

/w/   /j/   /j/

7. Wannaand Gonna

The two /t/ phonemes in "want to" can be linked to a single /t/ phoneme. The /u:/ is reduced to the schwa /ə/, and then many Americans drop the /t/ completely! A similar phenomenon occurs with "going to."

I want to go to Canada, because I'm going to go skiing.

wanna   gonna

8. Pausing

Native English speakers signal the end of one thought by pausing. Rising intonation indicates that the thought is not finished, but will be connected to a following thought. Falling intonation indicates that the thought is complete.

⇧   ⇧   ⇧   ⇩

I've been to London, Paris, Seoul, and Tokyo.

9. The Silent "h"

American English speakers are infamous for dropping "h's" in pronouns like "he," "him," and "her." When linked to proceeding words, these may often sound like "e," "im", "er." Note: this does not occur for all h-words like horse, horn, home, etc.

10. Emotion

This is often the hardest lesson for Chinese speakers of English. A statement (.) is usually indicated by falling intonation at the end of the sentence. A question (?) is normally indicated by rising intonation at the end of the sentence. An emphatic statement (!) is indicated through emphasis: louder, stronger, clearer speech.

She's not coming to the party.!?

> **Reflection:**
>
> If I had to rank the most important pronunciation lesson for Chinese learners, pausing would be near the top. What a difference it makes when students realize they are communicating real thoughts and meaningful sounds to an actual listener rather than rambling (or mumbling) into a void!

Where to Pause

One of the biggest factors in assessing someone's familiarity with English is to listen to how often and when they pause. Native English speakers will pause naturally at the end of each thought group. Commas (short pause with rising intonation) indicate the end of one yet-to-be-connected thought group; end punctuation (longer pause with falling intonation) indicates the end of one complete thought group.

⇧   ⇩
"We're leaving tomorrow," he said to the family. " We'll get to California in a few
⇩
months."

How to Pause

- pause at the end of each thought group
- lengthen the final syllable in each thought group
- rising intonation pitch at the end of the group
- falling intonation pitch at the end of a sentence

Chapter 13 Pronunciation

Listen to your instructor read the following equations. Can you hear the thought groups? Practice reading the equations with a partner. Your partner should point to the equation that you read.

1a) (A + B) - C = Y
1b) A + (B - C) = Y
2a) X + (Y x Z) = Q
2b) (X + Y) x Z = Q
3a) (A + B) - (C + D) + E = Z
3b) A + (B - C) + (D + E) = Z

Thought Groups

Commas and end punctuation are not the only places native English speakers will pause. The important thing to teach your students is that we pause at the end of one thought group. But how can we measure a thought? Isn't it subjective to label one group of words a thought and another group of words not a thought? Well, yes and no. Although individual readers may pause in different places, linguists have observed that native English speakers will typical pause (on average) in the same places and for the same reasons. The number one reason: to indicate the end of one thought group!

Take, for example, the following passage. I have marked where I would naturally pause when reading this passage. Most likely, your pausing is not too different. But do you know why we pause in these places? Try to give an explanation for each letter and why you would (or would not) pause at this place.

Scientists working in South America (a) have a really interesting job (b). The scientists say (c) that they must be very careful. (d) Sometimes (e) they study insects and animals (f) that are poisonous to humans.(g) It is really interesting for teachers to read stories about South American animals (h) and teach their students about them.

> Answers: (Don't read first!!!)
> a) - subject in the form of a long noun group
> b) - end of a sentence
> c) - reported speech (say, tell, report, explain)
> d) - end of a sentence
> e) - after an adverb which is in front of the subject
> f) - before a relative clause (who, that, which)
> g) - end of a sentence
> h) - at the end of a clause (between clauses)

Test Yourself

Read the following passage with a partner. Mark where you would pause and briefly explain why. Are there any places where you disagree?

Advertising a product in a different country can be very difficult. It can be very hard to translate and understand a culture. The product name and slogan are supposed to be great. That way people will want to buy it. However, sometimes the companies don't do enough research. The translated version of the slogan is wrong and sometimes offensive.

KFC (Kentucky Fried Chicken) tried to open some restaurants in China. Their award-winning slogan in the United States is "Finger-licking good." This means that the chicken is so delicious you will lick your fingers when you are done. When they translated this slogan into Chinese, it said, "You will eat your fingers off." Many people were surprised!

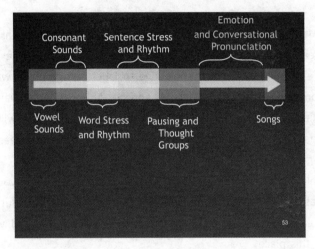

Emotional Adverbs

Getting students to recognize that when it comes to language emotion conveys just as much or meaning than the words themselves is a key lesson. Read the following question to a partner using a variety of the emotional adverbs listed below. Can you guess which emotion your partner is expressing?

Hi, what's your name?

Bored	Angry	Over-Interested	Shy	Worried
Pleased	Surprised	Arrogant	Disinterested	Drunk
Busy	Afraid	Upset	Embarrassed	Doubtful

Chapter 13 Pronunciation

> **Reflection:**
>
> I hate to say it, but many Chinese students too often view English as only a test subject—something to be memorized rather than used for the purpose of making friends, travelling, communicating experiences, etc. As such, the natural emotions, the variations in speed, and the different voices that humans use to communicate to other humans get left out of Chinese students' pronunciation all too often. This section contains some of my favorite and most popular activities to ensure that your students will view English as a fun, interesting, natural language and not just a test subject.

Guess Who?

Read the following dialogue with a partner in the voice of one the character pairs listed below. See if the pairs next to you can guess who is speaking.

> A: Hi, how are you?
> B: Fine, thank you. And you?
> A: Just great. What have you been doing lately?
> B: Oh, not much. But I've been keeping busy.
> A: Well . . . it's been good to see you.
> B: Yes, it has . . . well, bye!

1. Two boxers before a fight
2. Two spies
3. A divorced couple
4. A professor and his/her student
5. A couple in love
6. A mother and daughter
7. A psychiatrist and a patient
8. A serial killer and his victim
9. Two musicians in a band
10. Two telemarketers
11. Two siblings
12. The president of the U.S. and China
13. Two Shakespearean actors
14. Two newscasters
15. Two computer nerds
16. Mao Zedong and Zhou Enlai

Vocal Variety

As human beings with human emotions, we all speak differently at different times. Sometimes we speak loud; sometimes we speak softly; sometimes we speak quickly; sometimes we speak slowly; sometimes we are angry; sometimes are blissful. The meaning of words is often conveyed through our voice. Good speakers vary their speed, volume, and emotion to convey the proper meaning and grab the listener's attention. Bad speakers use a monotonous pattern or robotic, impersonal voice. Look at the short story below. Imagine you are reading this story to an audience of young children. Line by line consider the appropriate speed, volume, and emotion for each sentence. When finished practicing reading the story aloud to partners with their eyes closed.

>Weeks and months passed. (*slow and soft voice, a little tired*)
>There was very little food.
>Elizabeth was tired and hungry.
>"Will we ever get to California?" she asked her father.
>"Yes!" he said. "Be strong!!"
>Then one day, the wagon train stopped.
>It wasn't noon. It wasn't sunset!
>Elizabeth went to the front of the wagon.
>She saw a large green field.
>It was California!

Chunking

Pausing, emphasis, vocal variety, and proper emotion can make a huge difference in students' pronunciation. Read the following example below using effective pausing, emphasis, etc. and ineffective pausing, emphasis, etc. Do you hear the difference?

INTERESTING

Anyone can become a successful **teacher.**
but, of course,
the **unprepared**,
the **untrained**,
and those given too much **responsibility**
before they're **ready**
will **FAIL.**
That's what this morning's presentation is all **about.**

DULL

Anyone can become a successful teacher but of course the unprepared the untrained and those given too much responsibility before they're ready will fail that's what this morning's presentation is all about.

Look at the following extract. Read it aloud. Then, mark the pauses and highlight the stressed words. Your answers may differ from your partner's.

>There's one area of education where the best will always find a job. And it's so vital to the economy that its future is almost guaranteed. The true professional in this field has nothing to fear from technology or the changing marketplace. In fact, they can virtually name their own salary as they provide an essential service without which most economies would simply go out of business. I'm talking, of course, about teaching.

Chapter 13 Pronunciation

Sound Scripting

Professional speakers, newscaster, politicians, etc. will often sound script their speeches. A sound script is a written speech that incorporates pausing, emphasis, intonation, and emotional cues. Here's an example taken from *Presenting in English* by Mark Powell (Thomson Corporation):

> The **world's** most **popular DRINK**
> is **WATER**. (FACTUAL VOICE)
> You **probably knew** that **ALREADY**. (a little fast)
> After **all**,
> it's a basic **requirement** of **life** on **EARTH**. (long pause)
> But **did** you **KNOW** (gaining interest)
> that the world's **SECOND** most **popular drink**
> is **COKE**? (very interested)
> and that the human race drinks
> **Six hundred million Cokes a DAY**?(AMAZING!)
> Now, **let's** just **put** that into some **kind** of **PERSEPCTIVE**. (FAST)
> It **MEANS**
> that **EVERY WEEK**
> of **EVERY YEAR**
> people **drink** enough **COKE**
> to **fill** the **Empire State Building.** (slow and amazing!)
> **In FACT**,
> if **all** the **Coca-Cola** ever **CONSUMED**
> was **poured** over **Niagara FALLS**
> instead of **WATER**
> it would **take** nearly **TWO DAYS** to run **DRY**.
> There's almost nowhere on the **PLANET**
> from **MIAMI**
> to **MALAWI**,
> where the word **COKE**
> isn't **instantly RECOGNIZED**.
> The **brand name ALONE**
> is worth **THIRTY BILLION DOLLARS**.
> And that's what makes **COKE**
> a GLOBAL **MARKETING PHENOMENON**.

I will often have my students record their reading of the sound script above. Then, before they give a presentation before the class, I will ask them to write a sound script to consider their pausing, emphasis, emotion, etc. If your students aren't able to develop their own presentations, you can always ask them to sound script a page from the textbook or a dialogue from a novel.

> **Reflection:**
>
> Can you sing a song in another language? Maybe yes maybe no, but everyone would probably like to be able to sing a foreign song. Even if you are not the greatest singer or the world's greatest musician, your Chinese students will love to hear you sing. And, more importantly, you will be increasing their comfort level to take chances, speak louder, and sing along with you. Songs are great way to teach culture and create interest in the classroom, but they are also effective tools for emphasizing the pronunciation lessons covered in this chapter. Nearly any song can be used to reinforce pausing, emotion, rhythm, etc. Remember when choosing songs, it's best to build upon your students' interests—not your interests. You may not be a Lady Gaga fan, but if your students want to learn "Poker Face", why not? Remember you are teaching English, not music appreciation.

Here's one of my favorite songs and a good conclusion to this chapter. Remember: everyone has an accent and a different way of pronouncing phonemes. As long as we are tolerant of differences and listen to expand our own recognition of the variety among same sounds, we will improve as pronunciation teachers and in our relations with our students. Ultimately, pronunciation is easy to teach, but the hard for learners to apply. For this reason, stay cool and remember that the purpose of language is to communicate meaning not to speak like an American.

"Let's Call the Whole Thing Off"—George and Ira Gershwin, 1937.

You say either
And I say either.
You say neither
And I say neither.
Either either, neither neither
Let's call the whole thing off!
You like potato
And I like potato.
You like tomato
And I like tomato.
Potato potato, tomato tomato
Let's call the whole thing off!
But oh, if we call the whole thing off
Then we must part.
And oh, if we have to part
Then that would break my heart.

So if you like pajamas
And I like pajamas
I'll wear pajamas and give up pajamas.
For we know we need each other so we
Better call the calling off off.
Let's call the whole thing off!

Things have come to pretty pass
Our romance is growing flat
For you like this and the other
While I go for this and that.
Goodness knows what the end will be
For I don't know where I'm at
It looks as if we two will never be one.
Something must be done!

You like potatoes
And I like potatoes.

Chapter 13 Pronunciation

You like tomatoes
I like tomatoes.
Potatoes potatoes, tomatoes tomatoes.
Why don't we call the whole thing off?

You like bananas.
And I like bananas.
You like pajamas.
I like pajamas.
Bananas bananas, pajamas pajamas.
Why don't we call the whole thing off?

If you go for oysters
And I go for oysters,
I'll order oysters
And give up the oysters.
For we know we need each other so we
Better call the calling off off.
Let's call the whole thing off!
Let's call the whole thing off!
Let's call the whole thing off!

Reflection and Activity for Teachers

1. Translate the following words into their corresponding IPA symbols.

Face	Vase
Pass	Pest
Innovative	Motivated
Communication	Communism

2. Give 5 examples of a minimal pair and describe the difference in articulation for each pair.
3. Find a poem or song. Discuss with your partner what pronunciation lessons you could derive from the poem or song when teaching a TEFL course in China.
4. Sound script the following passage:

   Generating your own research questions is much more difficult than relying on your professor's prompt. However, it is also the first step to independent, analytical thinking, writing, and research! How can you design a research project that's never been done before? Hasn't everything been done before? Well, yes and no. Generating research questions is often easier than you may think. What's actually being asked of you is to read and understand the ongoing discussion within your field of interest. And then—and only then—to respond with your own opinions, observations, and arguments to that ongoing discussion.

5. Which of the exercises outlined in this chapter would work for the students you will be teaching? Which may to be too easy/difficult and need to be adapted? Think of two additional exercises to improve Chinese students' pronunciation.

Grammar-Based Lessons

Chapter 14

> The goals for this chapter are:
> ➢ To learn how to balance fluency and accuracy.
> ➢ To approach grammar through communicative language teaching.
> ➢ To design CLT materials and activities appropriate to the acquisition of TEFL grammar.

Communicative Language Teaching

Can grammar be taught in a more interesting and communicative manner than through the grammar translation method? While the acquisition of certain L2 grammatical rules is delayed (i.e., cannot be achieved overnight) in language learners, grammar can be taught through conversational practice and raising awareness of how accurately one speaks. It is important that students speak both **fluently** and **accurately**. Of course, lower-level learners will make frequent mistakes in their speech and may be unsure about which grammatical structures they have not fully acquired. As teachers we need to recognize the grammar lessons that our students have not acquired, so that we can (1) isolate the targeted grammar, (2) encourage students' to produce the targeted grammar, (3) create activities that allow students to practice and repeat the targeted grammar accurately, (4) correct and model proper usage and give proper feedback to students' errors, (5) develop implicit knowledge so that students can speak both fluently and accurately.

It's important to recognize the CLT also incorporates several checks for accuracy. During CLT, students learn to:

> ➢ ask questions for enhanced comprehension,
> ➢ listen actively and provide confirmations to other speakers
> ➢ ask for clarifications if the intended message is not received or misunderstood

Therefore, it is unrealistic to use a CLT approach toward teaching certain grammatical structures.

For example, let's imagine our students have been learning about count vs. non-count nouns.

Countable Nouns	Non-count nouns
desks, people, parking spaces	water, parking, pollution
many	much
few	little
there aren't enough	there isn't enough
fewer	less

How could we design a communicative activity that would reinforce the grammar learned?

Dialogues

One common approach to grammar-based communicative lesson planning is the use of dialogues that concentrate on the specific language goal. Although these dialogues may sound somewhat inauthentic, you are free to adapt these conversations and make them your own. For example:

Ke Xu: Why **are** there never **enough** taxis when you need one?
Bob: I know what you mean. **There's not enough** public transportation in this city.
Ke Xu: Yes and the subway's even worse. My god! I wish there were **more** subway lines.
Bob: The problem is **too many** cars and **too few** parking spaces. I used to drive into the city, but now it's so expensive.
Susan: Oh look! There goes another taxi. And it's full! Whew! Someone needs to talk to city hall.
Bob: That's a good idea. Why don't we get a cup of coffee and make a plan?

Dialogues are good for teaching natural intonation and rhythm in speech. I like to read the dialogue aloud line by line and have the students repeat after me, checking for pronunciation. Then, I have the students practice reading the dialogue twice with a partner, switching roles for the second reading. Now that students have acquired the language, we can go off the page and extend the dialogue. One option would be to create a similar, but more personalized and authentic conversation. I instruct students to create a similar dialogue, imagining that they and their partner are waiting for the bus or another form of public transportation. Or Bob and Ke Xu are now in the coffee shop and students create an entirely new dialogue that extends the previous conversation. While these new conversations are **open-ended** and allow for a multiplicity of personal responses, the students are hopefully focusing on the adjectives that precede count vs. non-count nouns. In other words, they are communicating freely but within a structured and targeted goal for their language use. We could follow-up this activity with a role play: students visit city hall to complain about public transportation. Students begin to listen and correct errors in count vs. non-count nouns. Or we complain about other subjects: poverty, war, commercials, etc., using the appropriate count vs. non-count adjectives. The important thing is that language acquisition—and especially syntactical formulations which may differ from students' L1—requires proper modeling, practice, feedback, more practice, error correction, and more practice.

This is not to say that a GTM-based approach is evil or unimportant in the acquisition of syntactical rules. However, repeated GTM-based approaches tend to depersonalize the lesson, reduce students' fluency, and lead to overreliance on teacher's feedback and correction. In fact, it may be a good idea to review long periods of interactive conversation with more independent, GTM-based exercises like the one below:

Read the following sentences and circle the correct answer.
- My apartment has too many/much furniture.
- There isn't/aren't enough water in California.
- I wish there were fewer/less police in my city.

Now write five sentences of your own.

Role-Plays

Role plays are a frequent component of CLT as they allow students to practice "authentic" language use within the safe confines of the classroom. Let's imagine we are teaching modals for politeness.
- Do it!
- Can you ....
- Could you ...
- Would you ...
- Might you...
- Would you mind + verb-ing (gerund) ...
- Please forgive me for asking, but would you mind...

Can you create a role play where students must produce questions and responses that focus on modals for politeness? For example:

Students are placed in groups of four and instructed to select a family member they wish to role play (e.g., grandmother, uncle, baby sister, family pet, etc.) All students must prepare three requests and commands for the other members of their family (e.g., Could you pick me up after school? Would you mind turning down your stereo? Stop smoking!). Students practice responding positively to polite requests and negatively to impolite commands. After 10 minutes of practice, select groups are chosen to perform their role-play in front of the class.

At the end, the teacher may call on other groups to summarize the other groups' role plays and offer comments.

Pacing of Grammar: A Natural Approach?

Teachers will occasionally ask me is there a naturally order in which L2 learners acquire English syntax? The simple answer to this question would be that everyone learns differently and at their own pace. However, this answer rarely satisfies those smart enough to ask this deceptively simple question. How can TEFL instructors determine which grammar lessons their students have already acquired and which they should next and in what order? Luckily, I have several practice ways to answer this question:

- ■Ask your students what they have learned.
- ■Consult the book they are using or have used and/or their Chinese instructors.
- ■Monitor your students and note which syntax they have acquired and which they haven't. As a native or near-native speaker of English you have credibility in recognizing what their major mistakes are.
- ■Follow the order below. Please note this should not be your first option and is based solely on my own TEFL teaching experiences without any research to support this order. This order should not be viewed as a dictum but as one man's simplified recommendations with several gaps and missing overlaps.

1. Who? Subjects —Vocabulary
    a. noun
    b. numbers
    c. adjectives
2. What? Verbs—Sentence Structure
    a. Simple Sentences
    b. Simple Sentence + Direct Object
    c. Simple Sentence + D.O. + I.O.
    d. Compound Sentence
3. When? Tense—
    a. Simple Present
        1. be verbs
        2. has/have do/does
        3. S-V agreement

    b. Simple Past
      1. -ed endings
      2. irregular verbs
    c. Present Progressive (be + verb-ing)
    d. Future Tense
  4. Where? Longer Sentences
    a. Prepositional phrases
    b. Perfect Tenses
    c. Sequence words (first, then, consequently, however)
    d. Articles
  5. Why? Complex Sentences
    a. Adverbs
    b. Subordinate Clauses (Because, as, although)
    c. Comparatives/superlatives
  6. How? Context
    a. Passive Voice
    b. Formal v. informal / Politeness cues
    c. Underlying meaning/tone
    d. Humor

Reflection and Activity for Teachers

1. Create a communicative activity that would reinforce students' acquisition of:
  a. Adverbs vs. Adjectives   b. He vs. she
  c. Relative Clauses (who, that, which...)   d. A, an, the, or nothing
  e. Question formation
2. Which is more important for your students: fluency or accuracy? How will you get your students to recognize the importance of both fluency and accuracy in their spoken English?

Grammar
Forms of Verb

- The infinitive—to be, to walk, to write, to eat
- Simple form—be, walk, write, eat
- Present tense—am, are, is; walk, walks; write, writes; eat, eats
- Past tense—was, were; walked; wrote; ate
- Present participle—being, walking, writing, eating
- Past participle—been, walked, wrote, ate

Present Continuous

- Combine "to be" with present participle:
  - I am walking
  - You are writing

- He is eating
- Meaning—right now or future
    - I am eating (right now as I speak)
    - I am eating lunch with my friend this afternoon.
    - He is going to Paris next week.

Simple Present

- 3rd person singular changes to agree with the subject
    - I write
    - You write
    - She writes
- Meaning—habitual, recurring action or future (with transportation or movement)
    - I walk to school every day. He eats lunch at that restaurant once a week.
    - The plane leaves at 10:30 tomorrow. She leaves for vacation next Friday.

Simple Past

- Regular and irregular verbs
    - I walked to the store this morning.
    - We wrote a letter to him.
- Meaning—action in the past, or something that is not real
    - If I had a million dollars, I would travel around the world.
    - I wish I were a grammar expert.

Past Continuous/Progressive

- Combine "to be" and present participle
- Meaning—one action was continuing while another action happened (may be implied)
    - I was eating when he arrived.
    - I couldn't answer the phone because I was taking a shower.

Modals

- Can, may, must, will, could, might, would, should
- Combine with the simple form of the verb (the infinitive without "to")
    - I may go to the movies
    - He can help you do that.
    - She should eat more vegetables.
- *Might, could, should,* and *would* are historically the past tense forms of *may, can, shall,* and *will*. Now "may" and "might" are interchangeable.
- "Could" and "would" often function as more polite forms.
- "Shall" is used more in British English than American to indicate a promise or make a suggestion.

Present Perfect

- Combine the auxiliary "have" with the past participle

- I have been to Rome.
- He has written the letter.
- Meaning—an action that started in the past and continues to the present.
- An action done repeatedly in the past.
- An action just completed.
- She has lived in China for 3 years. (action that started in the past and continues to the present)
- They have visited London several times. (action done repeatedly in the past)
- I have closed the door. (action just completed)

Past Perfect

- Combine "had" with past participle.
- Meaning—an action that occurred before another action in the past.
    - I had already eaten lunch when he invited me to go to the restaurant.
    - We had been there for an hour before they finally arrived.

Future

English has no future tense. Many forms can indicate future time:
- I am going there tomorrow.
- He may go next week.
- We will not forget.
- The train leaves in an hour.
- You can leave at 5:00.
- Look at the following dialog:
    - Mary: Are you going to the post office?
    - Sarah: Yes, I am.
    - Mary: Would you get me some stamps?
    - Sarah: Yes, I will.
- Can you exchange "will" and "going to" in this dialog? Is the meaning the same?

Will vs. Going to

- In both American and British English, the present continuous (be+verb+ing) is the most common way of referring to future time. The problem with teaching "will" as the future is that students then use it inappropriately—for example, they would say "I will go to visit my aunt next week" instead of "I'm going to visit my aunt next week."

Writing

Chapter 15

The goals for this chapter are:
- To question binary assumption regarding cultural difference between China and Western nations.
- To recognize and to avert signs of hostility in the acculturation process.
- To raise awareness of cultural differences and individual beliefs.

4 Modes of Language Learning

The four modes of language learning are reading, writing, speaking, and listening. Listening comes first. As a newborn baby, you spend the first year of life simply listening, absorbing sounds, and processing them through your normal mind before you even utter a sound. Listening is the first and usually easiest mode of language learning to teach. Second, comes speaking. Children around the age of one begin to master articulation of their lips, tongue, teeth, and vocal cords. Reading comes later and must be taught by parents, guardians, or teachers. This is because the written word is relatively new in evolutionary terms and is not naturally acquired by the human mind as of yet. The final mode of language learning is writing. For most TEFL students, writing is the most difficult mode of language learning to acquire. However, I like to say that writing is also the ultimate mode of language learning. Those who write well are usually good readers. Those who write well are usually good speakers. Those who write well listen well. If you can teach your students how to write in English, teaching them the other three modes of language learning will be a breeze!

Reinforcement

Unfortunately, writing will likely not be the primary focus of your TEFL teaching in China. Primary and middle school students largely do not possess the linguistic skills necessary to write extensively in English. Moreover, long-term TEFL writing instruction requires more time, material planning, and individualized feedback than may be practical for classes of 60+ students without prior writing instruction. For these reasons and more, most of the writing activities that you will be using in the China will serve to reinforce other modes of language learning. For example, a typical writing activity could reinforce a lesson on prepositions by asking students to compose six sentences of their own correctly using *on*, *in*, and *under*. Writing could be used to reinforce a listening activity by asking students to listen to a song while reading the lyrics and writing in the missing words. Writing can reinforce speaking, prompting students to take one minute before group discussions to write what they want to say or by writing a summary of what their group discussed. Writing can reinforce reading, requiring students to paraphrase a part of what they have just finished reading. In the alibi game I discussed in a previous chapter, writing could be used to reinforce speaking, listening, and grammar.

Alibi Game

Where were you last night between 7 and 11 pm?
Who were you with?
How did you get there?
When did you arrive?
When did you leave?
What did you see/buy/do?
Why did you go there?
Where did you go next?
What were you wearing?
Who saw you?

1. Students work in pairs to create the same alibi with as much detail as possible.
2. Then students are interviewed individually by a second pair acting as police. Answers given in complete sentences and past tense. Partners check for correct grammar.
3. Roles reverse and interviewees become police.
4. Police interview second pair (should have exact same alibi), asking same questions, and noting different and similar answers.
5. Each student files a written report of the differences and similarities between the two

Chapter 15 Writing

interviews, using complete sentences and past tense.

Writing Fluency

Assigning occasional writing tasks to your students can be a good—if not the best—way to improve their fluency. Using writing activities to build linguistic fluency implies that less attention will be given to accuracy or complexity. For the majority of your Chinese students, writing in English will be new and challenging. Getting students to perceive writing as fun and effective to improving their English is a worthwhile goal to set for any TEFL instructor. Below are some suggested ways to introduce the concept of building writing fluency in fun and interesting ways:

☐ **Autobiography Posters**

The Story of My Life

Ben was born in Pittsburgh, PA.
He has 1 brother and 1 sister.
His favorite sport is soccer.

☐ **Poems**

As in the example below poems can be a great way for students to introduce themselves. Teachers can also give instructions for individual lines or stanzas of the poem to teach parts of speech such as adjectives, relative noun clauses, and more.

Sally
Tall, studious, intelligent
Friend of Christine
Who loves music, books, and fresh air
Who is afraid of the dark, bad grades, and heights
Who wants to visit Brazil and France
Who likes to eat pizza
Resident of Shenzhen, China

☐ **Internet**

If your students have internet access, there are several useful sights to investigate, such as: chatrooms, class blogs, penpal.com, and email.

☐ **Haiku**

Haikus and similar poems can be a great way to introduce syllabication to your students. The example below asks students to write a poem that follows the pattern of thee syllables in the first line, one syllable in the second line, and five syllables in the third line.

A frog jumps.

Splash!

The sound of water.

☐ **Have You Seen**?

I use "Have You Seen" poems with students of nearly any level or age. One student acts as the camera while a second student acts as the photographer. The photographer positions the camera's head to take a three-second mental picture of an object inside or outside of the classroom once their shoulder has been tapped. The goal of these poems is for students to begin thinking in English, attempting to describe in words what they see, smell, taste, touch or hear.

Have you seen?	Have you seen?	Have you seen?
the bright red apple	my dead goldfish	a dog's eyes lighting up
sitting high in	at the top of the bowl	like black and green jewels
the tall, pale tree	floating in circles	its thick hair rising
way out of reach	and smelling of death	like a ladder
swinging in the slight breeze	Have you seen?	as it steps slowly forward?
Have you seen?		Have you seen?

☐ **Book Reports**

Many of your students may enjoy reading books in English during their free time. *Harry Potter* and *The Twilight Series* are perennial favorites throughout China. Students may want to present books they've enjoyed for recommendation to their classmates and teacher. Writing a book report is another great encourage to encourage students use of English for authentic purposes. For lower-level students, TEFL instructors may want to provide a prompt or outline, such as the one below, for writing a book report.

I read _____ by _____.

The story takes place in _____.

The main character was _____.

In the beginning, _____.

The most exciting part was _____.

At the end, _____.

The reason I like/dislike this book is _____.

☐ **Summaries and Paraphrases**

Nearly any classroom listening, speaking, or reading activity can be reinforced by asking students to write a summary or paraphrase of the material.

☐ **Mailbox**

Once a month students can write letters to a pen pal or another student in the class. Students can select their partners or teacher can pair students secretly. www.mylanguageexchange.com and other websites match second language learners searching for penpals for free.

Chapter 15 Writing

☐ Dear Laoshi,

A fun activity is to have students write to an expert for advice. Students can create real or fictional complaints, requests, invitations, etc. and reply in turn. Letter writing activities such as these can also be a good way to introduce formal and informal registers in English and politeness strategies.

> Dear Laoshi,
> Can you help me? I have a really big problem....

☐ Diary

Many TEFL instructors have asked students to keep a daily or weekly diary to help improve their English fluency. My own feelings about this approach are somewhat mixed. A diary is a great method for expanding one's abilities of self-expression; on the other hand, dictating to students to write and submit diary entries negates this primary benefit and may also expose you to submissions like the one below.

> August 13, 2010
> Dear diary,
>
> Today was a horrible day. I sat next to Billy in class and he punched me. I hate boys! I don't know why they are so mean. However, I am plotting my revenge. Tomorrow I will bring a knife to class...

☐ Language Learning Journal

A better suggestion than a personal diary is a language learning journal. Recently, I have begun using this method in my college courses to great success. A language cannot be learned only one hour a week in the classroom; students should be encouraged to study outside the classroom and practice the lessons from class. A language learning journal asks students to reflect on the lessons and then consider how they can practice the lesson outside of the classroom. For example:

> August 13, 2010
> Today in English class we learned about occupations. Occupation is another word for jobs. I learned the following vocabulary:
>
> | Mortician | starlet | electrician |
> | Director | plumber | undertaker |
>
> I think I did a good job remembering the vocabulary, but it was difficult to describe the occupations to my classmates. I should review adjectives like rich, famous, dirty, diligent in combination with these words more. I started to research possible occupations for my future in the library. I found several books written in about jobs in Hong Kong! Luckily, my English is now good enough to understand most of the words although I did have to use the dictionary at times. I spent two hours reading and studying in English and hope to learn more about a future career in electrical engineering!

◻ **Song Lyrics**

One of the difficulties teaching young adults is their disdain for newspapers, research articles, and literature. However, music seems to universally appeal to students age 13—18. Moreover, students love to show off their taste in music to their friends. As teachers, we can use this to our advantage by asking students to listen to songs and write the lyrics. We can also create humorous lyrics by changing those of existing songs. Finally, many TEFL instructors may have instrumental abilities. Bringing your guitar, keyboard, or violin to class is a great way to get students' attention. You can teach students a favorite song, or just play and ask students to write their own lyrics. Don't worry if your singing voice isn't Celine Dion quality; students will appreciate the effort regardless and you will be modeling how to overcome their fears speaking (or singing) in a foreign language.

◻ **Madlibs**

1. Only the prepositions have been erased from the essay below. Fill in the blanks using the proper prepositions.

_____ the early 20th century, Picasso divided his time _____ Barcelona and Paris. _____ 1904, _____ the middle _____ a storm, he met Fernande Olivier, a Bohemian artist who became his mistress. Olivier appears _____ many _____ his Rose period paintings. After acquiring fame and some fortune, Picasso left Olivier _____ Marcelle Humbert, whom he called Eva Gouel. Picasso included declarations _____ his love _____ Eva _____ many Cubist works. Picasso was devastated _____ her premature death _____ illness _____ the age _____ 30 _____ 1915.

2. Explain your choices.

3. All prepositional phrases (e.g., In the early twentieth century) have been removed from the following paragraph. Create your own prepositional phrases and position them at different locations in each sentence. Compare your writing with a partner.

Picasso divided his time. He met Fernande Olivier, a Bohemian artist who became his mistress. Olivier modeled for him. After acquiring fame and some fortune, Picasso left Olivier. He met Marcelle Humbert, whom he called Eva Gouel. Picasso dedicated many Cubist works to his love. When she died prematurely, Picasso was devastated.

◻ **Freewriting**

Freewriting also referred to as stream-of-consciousness writing is a strategy promoted by Peter Elbow (1975). This strategy works well as a way to gather ideas or just get your students' thoughts down on paper. Freewriting is more about fluency than accuracy or complexity. Students should be encouraged to write without correcting and to write as much as possible. You can also make this into a fun game by stopping students after a certain amount of time and having them count the number of words (usually at the bottom of the screen in an MS Word document). Students can keep a log of their average number of words per minute and try to increase their writing fluency.

I'm not sure wat I wanna write bout. Maybe I should write bout my favright ... uh, what's the word? Like something you uh like? Hobby... yeah, that's it. So, my favright hobby is soccer. In fact, I've plaid soccer since I was 8 years old. It's a great sport and my position is ... I don't know how to say in English but in Chinese its 守门员.

☐ Directed Freewriting

As many students have been grilled in the grammar-translation method of English language learning, they may not feel comfortable writing freely. Directed freewriting utilizes your students' grammatical strengths to develop their weakness in fluency and complexity.

1. Write a sentence:Dave swims.
2. Add an adverb: Dave swims slowly.
3. Add a prepositional phrase: Dave swims slowly in the sea.
4. Add adjectives: Daring Dave swims slowly in the deep, blue sea.
5. Add a second subject: Daring Dave and his faithful dog, Buck, slowly synchronize swim in the deep, blue sea.
6. Add an independent clause: Daring Dave and his faithful dog, Buck, slowly synchronize their swimming in the deep, blue sea; however, his wife, Maria, snores in her sleep.
7. Change the order of the clauses: While Maria, his wife, snores in her sleep, Dave who is daring and his dog, Buck, who is faithful, slowly, in the deep, blue sea, synchronize their swimming.

☐Collaborative Freewriting

A second option to freewriting, similar to the one above, is to have students collaborate to write longer and more complex sentences, paragraphs, stories, or essays. Place students into groups of 4~5 and follow instructions similar to those below:

1. Write a subject + verb. Pass clockwise.
2. Add a subject (Who?) Add an object (What?). Pass clockwise.
3. Combine sentences 1 & 3
4. Add an adverbial phrase (When?). Add a prepositional phrase (Where?). Pass clockwise.
5. Combine sentences 3 & 5.
6. Add an independent clause (Why?). Add a dependent clause (How?). Pass clockwise
7. Change the order of the word to create one clear sentence.

☐Picasso Freewriting

Having a model can help your students to see what authentic English writing looks like. You can copy any published piece of writing (following copyright laws, of course) and invite your students to follow the same sentence structure to create their own writing. For example:

Last week, the Bush administration put troubling distance between itself and principled Second Amendment defenders. We refer to the amicus brief that Solicitor General Paul Clement filed Friday in support of the plaintiffs in District of Columbia vs. Heller — the D.C. gun-ban challenge, widely expected to be the court's most significant gun-rights case in 60 years when a decision is reached (*Washington Times* , par.1).

Four hundred years ago, the Chinese emperor created new rules for peasants and principled servants. He posted the second law that his father created twenty years before in support of the farmers in Guangdong Province—the Rice Law, widely anticipated to be the founder's most exceptional agricultural ruling in the Ming Dynasty's history when a historical review is undertaken.

Plagiarism, Not Plagiarism?

Now might be a good time to discuss the issue of plagiarism. The biggest problem with the widespread GTM approach used throughout Chinese English classes is that students have few chances to write using their own words and ideas. This problem leads to numerous charges of plagiarism against Asian students studying at Western universities. While no one owns the English language—we all use the same words and basically have been exposed to many of the same ideas—the unacknowledged use of someone else's words and ideas is considered to be the ultimate form of disrespect. While your students may not be familiar with the rules of plagiarism, you can explain it as disrespect—or losing face—to copy without acknowledgment from the works of published authors, and in many cases is an illegal and punishable offense (although 100% unlikely it will go this far for you in Shenzhen). Of course, as can be seen in the example above borrowing the words and phrases of others can be a useful way to learn a language. The repetition of common knowledge or frequently used words or phrases in academic English is not considered plagiarism. For example, *Paris is the capital of France* is not my idea, but I would expect most readers to be familiar with it and you can find this easily 'fact' in multiple sources.

However, all other facts, words, or phrases that are not commonly known or used, and are not your own ideas or writing, must be cited. Here are some approaches to writing beginning with a plagiarizing approach and ending with an acceptable quoting technique. Where does plagiarism stop? Draw a line between the last approach that would produce plagiarism and the first approach that would produce acceptable original work.

1. Copying a paragraph as it is from the source without any acknowledgement.
2. Copying a paragraph making only small changes, such as replacing a few verbs or adjectives with synonyms.
3. Cutting and pasting a paragraph by using the sentences of the original but leaving one or two out, or by putting one or two sentences in a different order.
4. Composing a paragraph by taking short standard phrases from a number of sources and putting them together with some words of your own.
5. Paraphrasing a paragraph by rewriting with substantial changes in languages and organization, amount of detail, and examples, and citing the source.
6. Quoting a paragraph by placing it in block format with the source cited.

Chapter 15 Writing

Writing Is a Process

A popular *koan* among writing instructors is that writing is a process, not a product. Typically academic writing is divided into three stages: pre-writing, writing, and revisions. During the **pre-writing** stage, writers may brainstorm, freewrite, idea map, outline, read and note take, debate, role play, or just think quietly. During the **writing** stage, writers simply write without concern for errors of mistakes. They may leave blanks for words they can't think of (filling them in later with words from their vocabulary log, see Chapter 11). They may use "?" or "..." for parts they are unsure of are plan to add later; but the important thing is that students set aside a time and a place where they can write without interruption. During the final stage, **revision**, students can go back and check their grammar, vocabulary, organization, and specificity of their writing. Then, students may need to think some more, perform a second round of pre-writing strategies followed by more writing and more revision and on and on and on. In this way, a piece of writing never truly becomes a finished product and students learn how to break down the difficulty of writing is a step-by-step process.

    The concept of writing as a process may be new to your students. Chinese students commonly combine writing and revision into one step and largely do no pre-writing. This often leads to an arduous, time-consuming, physically and mental painful process for many Chinese writers of English. As a TEFL writing instructor, you can introduce and model pre-writing strategies (Picasso freewriting, directed outlines, idea mapping, etc.) which will likely be greatly appreciated by your students.

Error Correction

This subject will be covered in greater detail in the next chapter. For now, let's begin with a few basics. When it comes to teaching revision as part of the writing process, you should remind students that the burden for revision rests more upon their shoulders than upon yours. It would be quite time-consuming (not to mention ineffective) to revise 1000 student papers filled with syntactical and morphological errors. Remind students to separate writing from revision, take a break, grab a cup of tea before revising, and let them know it's natural and acceptable to make mistakes. A sign like the one below in the classroom or on the board can reinforce this idea:

I   MISTAKES!

Finally, you may want to provide some structure for revising related to lessons the students have previously acquired. For example, you can direct your student to correct only errors in subject-verb agreement, or errors in sentence construction, or errors in paragraph construction, etc. Encourage students to limit their revision to one or two key issues per page rather than marking everything in red. Students can also peer-review and correct each other's writing.

> **Reflection and Activity for Teachers**
>
> 1. How can you incorporate writing into a speaking and listening TEFL course without overwhelming yourself and your students?
> 2. With a partner devise another writing activity not included in this chapter that could help to build your students' writing fluency?

Error Correction

Chapter 16

The goals for this chapter are:
- To understand how and when to correct errors without losing face.
- To differentiate between errors and mistake.
- To encourage greater classroom fluency, accuracy, and complexity.

Correcting: Errors versus Mistakes

Everybody makes mistakes (especially, when it comes to second language learning). Mistakes are nature's signal that learning is taking place somewhere. Teachers who attempt to instill a fear of mistakes in their students are more likely instilling a fear of learning and life-long disdain for language, reading, and writing (Ferris 2002). So, never forget the #1 Rule:

■ Everybody makes mistakes!

An old joke queries, "How do you get to Carnegie Hall?" Answer: Practice, practice, practice. TEFL students need chances to PRACTICE the target language. In the classroom, you strongly encourage students' practice of the target language and reward positive or correct use. However, you would never PUNISH a student for making mistakes while practicing a second language, right?

■ If mistakes are repeated without recognition, then they may be errors.

Let's define **mistakes** and **errors**. According to *dictionary.com*, a **mistake** is "1. An error in action, calculation, opinion, or judgment caused by poor reasoning, carelessness, insufficient knowledge, etc. 2. A misunderstanding or misconception." An **error** is "1. A deviation from accuracy or correctness, 2. Belief in something untrue, 3. The condition of believing what is not true." These definitions for mistakes and errors tie-in nicely our previous investigations into language acquisition.

■ Errors in one language may not be errors in another language or dialect (i.e., direct translation).

Second language acquisition (SLA) theory predicts certain intra-language errors (e.g., Chinese speakers may use *he* and *she* indistinguishably). You'll hear plenty of mistakes and errors in a Chinese classroom of sixty or more students. As a second language learner yourself, study the differences and similarities between Chinese and English syntax, register, etc. The more you know about language(s), the better knowledge you will have to share with your students.

■ Be realistic in correcting errors: language is grown *i+1*, not instantly downloaded.

Yes, it would be great if our 12 year-old Chinese students could write like Walt Whitman and discuss language like Noam Chomsky. Unfortunately, this is an unrealistic expectation. Language acquisition is a step-by-step life-long process, not an internet download. Discuss your expectations with your students, co-workers, and fellow TEFL in China program attendees. Obviously, no TEFL instructor wants to be known as "Mr./Mrs. Drill Sargent", but imagine the extreme opposite: a classroom where errors are never corrected! Ahhhh!!!!

■ First, errors need to be pointed out.

Yes, people may not logically realize the errors they commit. A friendly and helpful tone of voice is a teacher's greatest asset when it comes to error correction. Better yet, train your students to correct each other's errors thereby saving you time and energy. It's important to review the chapter on Classroom Management for large classes and when and how to point out errors (see Saving Face section later). *For large classes:*(1) Get in the habit of keeping a notepad. (2) As you circulate record one or two frequently heard errors. (a) The best errors to correct are those related to the target language or skill. (b) The best errors to correct are those common to the class and not to one individual student. (c) The best errors to correct are those that your students can correct and raise their accuracy *i + 1*. (3) Write the error on the board. (4) Call on students to correct the error with help from the class.

■ Second, model correct usage.

Your attitude as a teacher greatly affects the attitude of the class. Likewise, you're speaking, listening, reading, and writing abilities greatly affect the English speaking, listening, reading, and writing abilities of your students. You are the primary model for your students English language learning. 120 eyes staring at you in expectation of linguistic perfection can be quite intimidating if your English is not of the Waldorf-Astoria sect. Good teachers practice their own speaking and listening skills before teaching these skills to others. A slight detour: this is why good teachers dress slightly nicer than their students and speak slight louder, slower, and clearer. You are a model for your students' learning! Act accordingly!

■ Third, how do you get to Carnegie Hall? Practice, practice, practice.
Yes, we discussed this one previously, but it bears repeating.

How do you know which is an error and which is a mistake?

If you are in this program, you are a Native-/Near-Native English Speaker (N/NES) with N/NES Credibility.

N/NES Credibility means that you're an English speaking, listening, reading, and writing expert (or at least expert for Chinese K-12 students). When you hear someone use English inaccurately, you know it! When you read an error in English print you recognize it! When you can't understand someone's English, the error is more likely than not in the other person's English rather than yours (perhaps except if you are from Wales, Newfoundland, or Texas!).

With N/NES Credibility you will recognize students' mistakes versus students' errors. If in doubt, short quizzes, interviews, or other forms of assessment can help you to isolate the errors your students are making.

Fluency over Accuracy

Teachers hoping to increase their students' communicative skills will refrain from interrupting their students every time they make a mistake. It is better to overlook problems with **accuracy** in order to facilitate the flow of speech, or **fluency**. While you want students to ultimately be both fluent and accurate, an overemphasis on accuracy will slow down the development of fluency because students will become nervous about speaking. Balance activities that focus on fluency with activities that focus on accuracy. In other words, encourage your students' attempts at speaking by guiding them unobtrusively and interrupting them only when comprehension is lacking, or if they repeat the same error again and again. Praise them regularly and lower their affective filters by encouraging all attempts at speaking.

> **Reflection and Activity for Teachers**
>
> 1. When is fluency more important than accuracy? When is accuracy more important than fluency? Explain.
> 2. What are some ways to give students feedback on accuracy without interrupting them?

Saving Face

No one likes to be corrected, especially in front of one's peers. The concept of face (see chapter on **Cultural Differences**) is important to Chinese and Westerners alike. Error correction can often be interpreted by students as linguistic behavior modification. For this reason, experienced TESOL instructors use games to correct students' errors. Games are great ways to make error correction more friendly and fun, and thereby more effective, but games introduce significant negatives as well: (1) Games often overemphasize accuracy at the expense of fluency; (2) Games tend to create an *us v. them* mentality in the classroom which can lead to superfluous, negative, or even abusive forms of error correction; (3) Games have *losers* and *winners* and are taken much more seriously than students than by teachers. In short, games are a double-edged sword. Be warned!

A better way to save face when it comes to error correction is to correct the class rather than individual students. This technique is especially for large classes. If you can correct an individual error to the benefit of the entire class, then do so without singling out the individual student. Don't stare down students, imitate them, or point them out to the class—don't single them out in front of their peers! Treat class errors not individual mistakes.

The best way to save face when it comes to error correction is to use the board. No classroom is complete with a board and some chalk. A computer screen and keyboard work equally well. First, write the error on the board. Second, model the correct use. Third, allow students the opportunity to correct themselves.

If you ever feel like you have *lost face* with one of your students, wait to assess the situation more deeply. *Losing face* can be simply interpreted as a lack of consideration for the other. The cure for losing face is to consider the person and assess their value more. As a result, effective error correction is more of a waiting game. You collect pieces of broken language, assess them, and try to piece them back together into a uniform whole. In practice, a student you call on makes an error. Her peers laugh and correct her error immediately. The student glares at you and you feel that you have done something to make this student *lose face*. Finally, you remember the TEFL training lesson that error treatment should focus on **reward** rather than **punishment**. When you pose a second question to the class, you immediately call on the glaring student and allow her to answer the easier question correctly. Thus, she beams with new language learning and face is saved.

Error Treatment

Stay positive when treating errors. Remember critical feedback is best received when it is offered with a dash of support and motivation. The most critical errors to treat are those that result in communication problems (save the lessons on *a*, *an*, and *the* for advanced classes). I have categorized into my targeted skill lessons: introductions, asking follow-up questions, debate strategies, changing the topic, etc.

Try to limit your error correction to linguistic errors and avoid correction of behavior, dress, appearance, or culture. Be especially aware of over-correcting students' pronunciation.

Ask your students how much correction they want. You may be surprised to learn that many advanced ESOL learners want to be corrected and appreciate individualized feedback. While class size, level, and mood can affect the detail of error treatment expected from the instructor, this is something you may want to discuss with your class. Consider the pros and cons of treating errors individually or collectively.

Feedback in the Classroom

Effective teachers teach their students who to correct each other's and their own errors. Here's some useful vocabulary related to the discussion of feedback:

- **explicit correction**: teacher provides correct form
- **recasts**: teacher reformulates all or part of student utterance, generally implicit
- **clarification requests**: indicates misunderstood utterance, ill-formed utterance
- **metalinguistic feedback**: does not provide explicit instruction, but asks learner to consider the linguistic correctness of the past statement
- **elicitation**: questions, finishing a sentence (he likes to what?), or reformulation of utterance
- **repetition**: repetition of student error with intonation to highlight it.

Recasts are most common (50% of the time), followed by elicitations, clarifications, metalinguistic feedback, explicit correction, and repetition.

The least likely form of feedback by which students acquire the target language or skill is recasts. The highest positive correlation between feedback and language acquisition are elicitations, clarifications, metalinguistic feedback, and repetition.

Reflection and Activity for Teachers

1. In groups of 4 or 5 practice making and correcting simple linguistic errors.
2. Take turns comparing clarification requests, metalinguistic feedback, elicitation, repetition, recasts, and explicit correction. Which of these methods would work best for your class? Why?
3. What problems do you anticipate with error correction and/or saving face in the Chinese classroom? Discuss.

Cultural Differences

Chapter 17

The goals for this chapter are:
- To question binary assumption regarding cultural difference between China and Western nations.
- To recognize and to avert signs of hostility in the acculturation process.
- To raise awareness of cultural differences and individual beliefs.

"You don't understand the basic assumptions of your own culture if your own culture is the only culture you know... Everybody operates on certain basic assumptions, but very few people know what those assumptions are... The only way you find out is by contrasting the way you look at something to the way it is looked at in another culture."

— Alan Watts, *The Tao of Philosophy*

How Can an Outsider Assess Another's Culture?

If this is your first trip to China, you probably feel like you landed in another world. We began this textbook by discussing your expectations for living in China. Some of your expectations were probably to learn a new language and a new culture. But what is culture? *Dictionary.com* defines culture as "the behaviors and beliefs characteristic of a particular social, ethnic, or age group." Even if you feel like inherently connected to a particular social, ethnic, or age group, it's

Chapter 17 Cultural Differences

important to recognize that your individual behaviors and beliefs likely differ significantly from others in your group. What's more, among the 1.4 billion Chinese on Earth individual behavior and beliefs can differ dramatically. We all know this, but at some point over the course of the next year some of you will forget this important point. In fact, I can almost guarantee that it will happen to an overwhelming majority of those new to the Chinese culture. I can make this guarantee because it happened to me and it's a natural result of acculturation.

Tourists to foreign countries will regale you with exotic tales of how differently the people acted and thought. New TEFL teachers who live for one year in a foreign country will expertly document and explain how the two cultures differ. But talk to someone who has lived in the culture for decades, speaks the language fluently, and has married into or adopted a second family in a new culture, and you may hear something quite unexpected: cultural similarities. Living in Asia for nearly seven years, I can tell you that my lifestyle was relatively similar to what it would have been if I had remained in the U.S. during this period. I ate three meals most days, studied in my free time, practiced guitar, went to the gym, went to restaurants and occasional house parties with my friends, had both long- and short-term relationships, breathed in and out, and talked to people as my equals. Perhaps I walked a bit more and ate slightly fewer Twinkies than I otherwise would have. In other words, I found many more similarities than differences. I freely and individually chose my job, my friends, and the overwhelming majority of my interactions just as if I were living anywhere else on Earth. There were certain aspects of Chinese culture that I agreed with and chose to follow and certain aspects of Chinese culture that I disagreed with and chose not to follow just as I had done with American culture. I had gone to China to learn the language and its culture, but along the way I ended learning about myself, my culture, and the similarities of people of the world share.

Self-Assessment

Take a few minutes to write certain traits that describe culture in China compared to culture in your home country. Don't worry, these notes will not be shared with the class, but will be retained for your own personal records only.

Chinese   American/Western

-
-
-
-
-

Conventional Cultural Difference

TEFL education prior to the 1980s was plagued by cultural stereotypes and overgeneralizations.

It's not hard to find binary categorizations like the following:

Collectivist	*Individualist*
traditional	*modern*
small groups	*large groups*
harmony	*debate*
modesty	*assertiveness*
prestige from others	*self-respect*
high power distance	*low power distance*
high context	*low context*
uncertainty avoidance	*uncertainty acceptance*

High Context vs. Low-Context

Anthropologists place cultures on a scale from low context to high context. Members of high context cultures share:

- ★ Religion
- ★ Socioeconomic status
- ★ Education background
- ★ Ethnicity
- ★ Cultural practices

Members of low context cultures come from different ethnic, religious, educational and socioeconomic backgrounds. As a result they tend to differ widely on:

- ★ Values
- ★ Attitudes
- ★ Beliefs

As a result, low context cultures tend to value:

- ★ Written communication over oral (more has to be explained to people who don't share your background),
- ★ Individual achievement over group welfare,
- ★ Separation of work and personal life,
- ★ A democratic workplace structure,
- ★ Competition and aggression.

Both America and China, while very much a low context culture in some ways, operate as a high context culture in others. For example, you may find that people at your school tend to:

- ★ Disseminate information orally rather than in writing,
- ★ See a close relationship between your behavior as a teacher and your behavior outside school hours,

- ★ Avoid conflict and direct confrontation with you when there is a disagreement,
- ★ Expect you to live with the current situation rather than trying to make changes.

Power Distance

Power distance in a workplace that values input from all is low, resulting in a tendency for leaders to consult subordinates on decisions, a negative regard for close supervision, and an emphasis on equality in the workplace. In a culture with high **power distance**, employees will be more closely supervised, not consulted in decision making, given unequal privileges, and less likely to trust each other.

Uncertainty Avoidance

Cultures with a low degree of Uncertainty Avoidance result in acceptance of diversity in thought and behavior, low resistance to change and a strong achievement motivation. In a culture with a high degree of Uncertainty Avoidance, strict laws and norms minimize anxiety, group decision-making is favored so no one takes the risk of responsibility, there is emotional resistance to change, and there is weak achievement motivation.

Individualism

Cultures with a high regard for individualism result in the expectation for people to take care of themselves, small nuclear families, little emotional dependence on the employer, individual decision-making, and motivation coming from individual desires. In a culture with a low regard for individualism, loyalties will be primarily to the family, close friends and possibly the workgroup, there is strong loyalty and emotional dependence on the employer, an emphasis on conformity and orderliness.

Assertiveness

Cultures that value assertiveness emphasize competition, earnings, recognition and achievement, high job stress, and the centrality of work. A culture that does not value assertiveness sees work as less central to life, defines achievement in terms of human relationships, values fewer work hours over higher salaries, resulting in lower job stress.

Dealing with Cultural Problems in the Workplace

You can minimize problems by:

- ★ Working closely with the other teachers so that you are included in information-sharing
- ★ "Triangulating" any requests or complaints by having a 3rd person present them for you—that way, you do not risk conflict with the other party.
- ★ Accepting that there may be valid reasons for the way things are done, even if you don't understand what they are.
- ★ Think of yourself as a role model for the students wherever you are.

Four Stages of Acculturation

(1) <u>Honeymoon</u>—characterized by excitement, anticipation, enjoyment of differences.
(2) <u>Hostility</u>—characterized by irritation, anger, depression, physical ailments.
(3) <u>Humor</u>—characterized by a growing ability to deal with the differences and see them as interesting or funny.
(4) <u>Home</u>—characterized by the ability to function well and feel comfortable in the new culture.

The hostility stage of acculturation can be quite difficult and even dangerous. It is caused by the tension between changing your actions to fit into the new culture and holding on to aspects of your identity. It's important to recognize that everyone living in and attempting to adapt to a new culture will at some point pass through the hostility stage and for many this stage will last for a significant period of time.

Symptoms include:

- ★ Anger toward members of the new culture
- ★ Anger toward members of your old culture
- ★ Tiredness, depression, feeling that living in the new culture is too hard
- ★ Physical symptoms such as headaches, digestive problems, sleep disorders

You should keep an eye not only on yourself but also your friends and colleagues in the program for repeated occurrences of these symptoms. The best way to overcome feelings of hostility toward your new culture is to have the support of your peers, co-workers, and the CTLC program. Understanding the cause of these symptoms and knowing that they are temporary can help you deal with them. Other suggestions:

- ★ Stay in touch with family and friends through email, letters, and phone. Tell them about your experiences.
- ★ Form an informal support group with others from your own culture to share feelings and ideas for adjusting to the culture.
- ★ Find some activities in the new culture that you enjoy and do them often.
- ★ If you see others becoming angry or retreating into depression, plan an activity with them and try to remind them of the positive aspects of living in a new culture. (Do not tell them they are in culture shock! That just makes the situation worse.)

Chapter 17 Cultural Differences

Resolving Workplace Cultural Differences

The biggest joy of TEFL teaching is that you are instantly accepted into a foreign community. Take pride in the fact that you are not just a tourist passing through, but a member of a professional community. Your co-workers, colleagues, and students will want to see that you appreciate being invited into their community. Imagine if you invited someone into your home for a year and they never wanted to talk with you or spend personal time getting to know you better. Most differences can be resolved simply by talking and showing a sincere interest in those you come into contact with. Of course, this does not mean that you must abandon your personality, beliefs, or desires. A community is still comprised of individuals. However, the effort you put into becoming a full-fledged member of your community will go a long toward resolving the inevitable bumps along the way. Here are a few easy-to-follow methods for establishing yourself as a community member rather than an interloper:

- Talk to your co-workers. Tell them how your teaching style and methods may differ from theirs. TEFL conversation classes of 60+ students can grow loud at times!!!
- Observe your co-workers. Visit their classes (always ask permission beforehand, of course) and take note of their strengths and weakness. Share your observations in a helpful but frank way. Encourage them to do the same for you.
- Maintain regular office hours. Let your co-workers see you in the office, preparing for your classes, and take your work responsibilities seriously.
- Attend departmental or campus meetings, participate in festivals, play sports, and eat with your students and co-workers.
- Recognize the stage of hostility in yourself; let your colleagues know when you are feeling angry, sad, or alienated, communicate openly and honestly about your attitude with those closest to you.
- Recognize the stage of hostility in others, seek to help them in overcoming their struggles or lend a friendly ear.

Reflection and Activity for Teachers

1. Your students are likely interested in your background and your culture. How will you introduce your beliefs and culture to your students? Share your answers with a small group.
2. Create a role play centering upon one cultural difference that you predict to encounter in your new workplace. Attempt to resolve the situation peacefully and intelligently using the information acquired in this chapter. [15 minutes]

English in China's Educational System

Chapter 18

By Liu Shusen, Ph. D., Professor and Associate Dean, School of Foreign Languages, Peking University

> The goals for this chapter are:
> - To describe briefly the position of English in China's educational system
> - To understand the goals of teaching English to Chinese students
> - To explain how English is taught at schools and colleges
> - To introduce the assessment of the performance of English teachers
> - To describe the teaching of spoken English by native speakers of English

The Position of English in China's Educational System

As a country of fifty-six ethnic groups, China is composed of peoples speaking more than eighty dialects and languages, over thirty of which have their own written forms. Thus governmental policies on languages are of vital importance in China, especially since the late 1970's when China initiated its "reform and open-up" policy.

The history of teaching English at public schools and institutes in China can be traced back to 1862, when the first early modern public school of foreign languages in China, Tongwen Guan, was established in Beijing. But the nationwide popularity of teaching the English language did not

Chapter 18 English in China's Educational System

come until the 1990's, when the Ministry of Education constituted the policy of teaching English as a compulsory course for every level, from primary schools to doctoral programs.

In economically and culturally developed cities such as Beijing, Shanghai and Shenzhen, English is a required course beginning in the first year of primary school. In many cities and regions English is a compulsory course from the third year of primary school.

The entrance examinations and graduation examinations from middle schools to colleges and even postgraduate programs are officially required to include a test of English. There are now more than 200 million people leaning English in kindergartens, schools, colleges and private training schools in China.

Goals of Teaching English in China's Primary and Middle Schools

Primary school education in China consists of six years, and the legal age for entering primary school is six. It is followed by "middle school" education, equivalent to secondary education, which includes junior high school and senior high school. But the system divides the six years of middle school education into two phases. The first three years are compulsory nationwide; the second three years are senior high school, and are not compulsory.

As a national policy, China regulates the system of a nine-year compulsory education throughout the county, which extends from primary school to middle school (junior high school). English is a required course in this system of the compulsory education, and it remains so in senior high school.

In the early 1990's the Ministry of Education issued general outlines to provide general principles and comprehensive regulations for the teaching of English in primary schools and middle schools. Since then those outlines have been popularly used in all the public primary schools and middle schools, as guides for both teaching English and assessing the outcome of teaching and learning of English.

The general outline for teaching English in primary schools requires that standard time for the first and second years be a total of 175 teaching hours, on the average of five teaching hours/ week in 70 weeks, when pupils are expected to learn 400 English words. The total of the standard time for the third to the sixth year is 560 teaching hours, on the average of four teaching hours/week in 140 weeks. By the end of the sixth school year, pupils are expected to learn 1,200 English words, 450 of which they should be able to spell and use in both speaking and writing. The outline also introduces the basic knowledge of English grammar such as essential sentence structures and commonly used tenses, which should be taught consecutively in six years of primary school.

The general outline for teaching English at middle schools (junior high schools) requires that the minimum time for teaching English be four teaching hours per week. The outline is composed of two sets of teaching goals, in the light of the teaching conditions at different schools. The lower set of teaching goals expects students to learn 450 English words and 100 idiomatic phrases in three years, building on the English teaching in primary schools. The higher set of teaching goal expects students to learn 800 English words and 200 idiomatic phrases in three years. In addition, the students are required to read extracurricular English materials totaling as much as 100,000 words in three years. The standard speed of reading English for them to reach is 50 ~ 70 words per minute. The standard speed of writing in English is 10 ~ 12 words per minute.

For senior high schools, which are beyond compulsory education, the general outline for teaching English differs significantly from the other two outlines by a three-fold increase in the minimum time for teaching English, to 12 teaching hours per week, for a total of 384 teaching hours in three school years.

The senior high school outline is also composed of two sets of teaching goals in the light of the teaching conditions at different schools. Both sets of goals expect students to learn 750 English words and idiomatic phrases in three years, adding to the 1,200 English words the students should have learned in primary and middle school. The students are expected to attain a reading speed of 80 words per minute. The standard for speed of writing in English is 15 words per minute. In addition, they are required to read extracurricular English materials totaling as much as 100,000 words in three years according to the lower set of teaching goals or 200,000 words according to the higher set of teaching goals. The higher set of teaching goals further expects students to be able to write a paper of 80 ~ 100 English words within 30 minutes.

Principles for Teaching English in Schools and Colleges

Generally speaking, at schools and colleges in China since the 1950's there has been an emphasis on having the students of English be taught so as to develop equally well in five kinds of abilities of using the language: listening, speaking, reading, writing, and translating between English and Chinese. That emphasis is also applicable for the teaching and learning of all the other foreign languages in China.

The principles, which are consistent with the cultural heritage of perfectionism or idealism in Chinese education, are intended to develop the English proficiency of Chinese students to be equal to native speakers of English, and perhaps even to exceed the language skills of monolingual native speakers of English, who have little or nothing to do with bilingual translation.

In spite of the popularity of those principles as the nationally accepted goals for teaching English and other foreign languages, the teaching and learning of English naturally has different focuses in primary schools, middle schools and colleges, as students differ a lot in age, in their goals of learning English, and in their language acquisition ability. In primary schools during the first two years the emphasis is on listening and speaking. Then from the third through the fifth year of primary school the listening, speaking, reading, and writing are equally emphasized. In the sixth year of primary school the ability of bilingual translation between English and Chinese is added into the requirements.

From junior high school to senior high school, as the students learn more words and grammar, the ability of listening, speaking, reading, writing and translating are increasingly stressed for the students to reach higher levels, according to the outline by the Ministry of Education. But in reality, teachers of English and students tend to pay more attention to the ability of reading, writing and translating, and much less to listening and speaking. The reason is that the English tests primarily use written questions, with only with a small part for testing a student's listening ability. Very few English tests in junior and senior high schools assess the student's ability in speaking.

The general neglect of developing the skills of speaking English is that teachers and students have to strive for higher scores in the increasingly competitive situation of education. The examination scores are decisive for a student's application for schools and colleges with better prestige and a higher quality of education. The students' scores are also decisive for the professional assessment of their teachers, overshadowing all other aspects of their teaching performance. However, in recent years the consequence of that neglect of developing the English speaking skills has been that Chinese students are conspicuously strong in their ability of reading and writing and bilingual translating, but almost universally weak in speaking English. The students even call themselves "dumb" learners of English, as in "deaf and dumb". Such an unbalanced situation has caught the attention of scholars, educators, and the policy makers at various levels of governmental administration. Efforts are being made to call more attention to promoting the ability of speaking English so as to be on par with listening, reading, writing and translating. One of the administrative efforts to begin correcting that unbalance in teaching and learning of English has been a gradual increase in assessing English listening and speaking ability in English examinations at all levels.

Assessment of the Performance of English Teachers

The assessment of the performance of English teachers in primary and middle schools and in colleges is the same as for the teachers of all the other subjects. Assessment is usually made on annual basis in accordance of two principles: the administrative regulations of the school where the teacher of English works and the general outline by the Ministry of Education for the supervision of teaching English as a specific subject. However for new teachers, the assessment may be made monthly or even weekly depending on the actual performance of the teacher.

The assessment includes such major areas as teachers' professional qualifications, working attitude and performance, completion of assigned teaching loads, self-evaluation, public contributions, peer comments, and students' evaluation, which is made by anonymous questionnaires. Each student is required to fill in an individual questionnaire at the end of a semester or school year.

Assessment is compulsory for all teachers, but the results are used only as reference for the survey and improvement of the teaching quality, unless an individual teacher's performance is much below the basic requirements or if there is concern about some serious mistake or misconduct.

Teaching of Spoken English by Native Speakers of English

According to the statistical report of the Ministry of Education in 2010, in mainland China there were 290,597 primary schools, 85,132 middle schools (including junior and senior high schools), and 2,358 colleges and universities. Although no statistics is released on the total number of foreign teachers employed as native speakers in Chinese schools, colleges and universities, the general estimate is that foreign teachers comprise less than one percent of all the teachers of English nationwide. The percentages of foreign teachers as native speakers in colleges and universities, where the foreign teachers mainly teach students who are English majors in the Department of Foreign Languages, is much higher than in primary and middle schools. And among primary and middle schools, the percentage of foreign teachers as native speakers is higher in urban areas than in rural areas.

In developed cities such as Beijing and Shanghai, about 10 percent of the primary schools and 15 percent of the middle schools employ foreign teachers as native speakers of English. Some of the primary schools in Beijing employ foreign teachers as native speakers of English to teach the pupils from the first school year. Furthermore, in recent years parents have been developing an increasingly strong interest in sending their children to private part-time English schools where the children can learn English naturally and idiomatically, often preferably learning conversational or spoken English, under foreign teachers who are native speakers of English, sometimes even in one-on-one tutoring.

Foreign teachers who are native speakers of English usually teach courses of spoken English that are supplementary to the regular English courses that focus on training the ability of listening, reading, writing, and translating between English and Chinese. In most cases, students can have access to one or two English classes a week taught by native speakers of English. Such courses usually have separate textbooks, which the teachers use to stress the training of English pronunciation and intonation, conversational skills, sentence patterns and idiomatic phrases for specific scenes of social communications.

Chinese students often have an interest in the otherness of English language and culture, and so they are prone to prefer learning spoken English from native speakers, trusting them for their idiomatic use of the language and cultural knowledge. The spoken English classes taught by native speakers of English also seem to develop and promote the students' interest in learning English more readily than do their Chinese colleagues, because the regular English courses, aimed at the examinations, necessarily assign homework that is more time-consuming and perhaps less interesting.

It has turned out to be a welcome trend in schools with foreign teachers as native speakers of English, that the effective cooperation of a foreign teacher with his/her Chinese colleagues can have a highly favorable impact on the Chinese students of English, especially in spoken English, but which also extends to the regular English classes. The people-to-people classroom communication with the foreign teachers provides an opportunity for a natural and intuitive way of understanding the English language and culture.

Living and Teaching in China: Tips for Teachers

Chapter 19

By De-an Wu Swihart, Ph. D. & William O'Donnell, Ph. D., Co-Directors, Center for Teaching & Learning in China

CHINESE EDUCATION

The School System in China
- Elementary schools (xiaoxue): grades 1-6 = U.S. grades 1-6 (ages 6-11)
- Middle School (chuzhong): Junior 1-3 = U.S. grades 7-9 (ages 12-14)
- High School (gaozhong): Senior 1-3 = U.S. grades 10-12 (ages 15-17)
- Secondary schools (zhongxue)
- Two-year professional training schools, as an alternative to high school (zhongzhuan)
- Three-year professional training colleges (dazhuan)
- Four-year colleges and universities (daxue), some of which are specialized professional colleges, such as the Beijing Foreign Language University (for training foreign-language experts) and Beijing Normal University (for training teachers).

Administrative Organization of Elementary and Secondary Schools

The Secretary of the General Party Branch (dang zongzhi shiji) is the official head of the school; in most schools the principal also holds this post. The principal (xiaozhang) makes all the final decisions at the school. The vice-principal (fu xiaozhang) is in charge of the day-to-day administration of the school. Department chairs (xueke zuzhang) are in charge of a subject area, such as English, Math, Chinese. The Office of Educational Administration (jiaowu chu) is in charge of faculty, curricula, teaching materials, examinations, student records, and the school library. The Office of Student Affairs (xuesheng chu) is in charge of student affairs and counselling.

National College Entrance Examinations

National college entrance examinations are held every year in June for high school graduating seniors. All of the students take the examinations in Mathematics, English, and Chinese. Science students also take exams in Physics, Biology, and Chemistry. Humanities and Social Science students also take examinations in Political Science, Geography, and History. The National Examinations Authority of the Ministry of Education sets all the exam questions. The examination papers are sealed and sent to examination halls all over China the day before the examinations start. Students who do not pass the national examination may take it again the next year or go to professional schools. Because of intense competition in the college entrance examinations, many secondary school students, especially high school seniors, get extra tutoring after school and during vacations. Schools give several practice entrance examinations to their students. Because of the importance of the national college entrance examinations, secondary schools in China strictly follow study guidelines from the Ministry of Education and focus on preparing their students for the examinations. Students who pass the national entrance examinations and get into college usually can graduate after four years of study. The government used to provide centralized job placement for every college graduate, but now the government lets college graduates find jobs themselves, and the government no longer guarantees job placement.

Key Secondary Schools and Universities

Some Chinese secondary schools and universities are designated as "key" schools (zhongdian xuexiao) by the central or regional government and receive extra funding to provide better teaching facilities and to hire the best teachers. The "key" universities are allowed to recruit the best students from the National Entrance Exam. Those schools and universities have higher admission standards and are expected to produce excellent graduates.

Chapter 19 Living and Teaching in China: Tips for Teachers

Typical School Calendar in China

September 1: Fall semester begins

September 10: Teacher's Day

October 1: National Day (one week)

January or February: Winter vacation (three or four weeks, usually beginning about ten days before the Chinese New Year, which is also called Spring Festival, and usually ending after the Lantern Festival)

Mid-/Late February: Spring semester begins

March 8: International Women's Day (one day)

April or early May: Qingming Festival (one day)

May 1: Labor Day (usually about three days)

June 1: Children's Day (one day)

Approximately July 10—August 31: Summer vacation

Typical Daily Schedule for a Chinese School (each school will vary somewhat)

Morning

6:20-6:40 a.m. Morning exercises

6:40-7:10   Breakfast

7:30-8:10   First period

8:20-9:00   Second period

9:00-9:40   Third period

9:40-10:10   Break, exercises

10:10-10:50   Fourth period

10:50-11:10   Eye-health exercises

11:10-11:50   Fifth period

Midday

11:50-12:20 p.m. Lunch

12:20-1:50   Middaybreak

Afternoon

1:50   Wakeup

1:55   Five-minute warning bell

2:00-2:40   Sixth period

2:50-3:30   Seventh period

3:40-4:20   Eighth period

4:30-5:30   Extracurricular activities

5:30   Dinner

Evening

6:45-7:45   Self-study

7:45-8:00   Break

8:00-9:30   Self-study

PEOPLE AND CUSTOMS

How to Address People

To address a person senior to you in age or rank, add the person's title after his/her surname. For example: "Wáng Zǒng" for CEO Wang, "Lǐ Jīnglǐ" for manager Li, "Zhāng Lǎoshī" for teacher (or professor) Zhang. To address your peers, colleagues, or friends, you can add "xiǎo" or "lǎo" before their surname. For example: Xiǎo Wáng, Lǎo Zhāng.

To address people whom you don't know, you call a young lady "xiǎojiě," call a man "xiānsheng," and call working people (cooks, drivers, etc.) "shīfu." "Tóngzhì" (comrade) is still used to address both men and women whom you don't know, but has become much less common.

Unexpected Visits to Your Home

In China it is a common practice for relatives, neighbors, or friends to visit without calling first. If a guest suddenly appears at your door, you usually should invite him or her in. If you are really busy at that time, you can politely say sorry and that he or she is welcome to come back some other time.

Family Dinners

If you are invited to the home of a friend or colleague for dinner, you should take a gift (fruit, wine, flowers, candy, cake, or toys for children). The etiquette at a family dinner is less formal than at a banquet. The host might ask you to sit at a special place or simply have you sit wherever you choose. A finger towel might be offered or there might only be napkins. There will be formal toasts before the dinner begins. The host usually takes some food from the dishes on the table and puts it on your plate. It is impolite to refuse to eat it.

Gifts in China

Choosing a gift

When giving gifts in China, consider both the occasion and the recipient. If you are going to visit a family, small gifts such as flowers, fruit, and local special products are appropriate. If the family has children, candy and toys will be appreciated. For important holidays, such as Chinese New Year (the Spring Festival), women can be given perfume, makeup, clothing, etc. while for men, wine, liquor, tea, wallets, belts, etc. are good choices.

But you need to be careful to avoid certain tabooed gifts: Old people shouldn't be given clocks, because clock "zhōng 钟" has the same pronunciation as "zhōng 终", meaning "death." Similarly, you shouldn't give umbrellas to couples, because "sǎn 伞" (umbrella) sounds like "sǎn

Chapter 19 Living and Teaching in China: Tips for Teachers

散", one of whose meanings is "to split up." Nor should you give pears (lí 梨) to a married couple, since it sounds like "lí 离" (to leave, apart). For weddings always give paired gifts; the Chinese say: Hǎoshì chéng shuāng 好事成双 "good things come in pairs" and so a gift without its pair suggests separation or divorce.

Chinese don't like white or black colored gifts or wrapping paper because those colors symbolize or suggest sadness, poverty, bad luck, or disaster. On the other hand, the color red symbolizes happiness, joy, luck and good fortune, so red wrapping paper is desirable.

Occasions for giving gifts in China

Teacher's Day (September 10)
Chinese New Year/Spring Festival (January—February)
Birthday
Wedding
Graduation
First time visiting the parents of a friend, especially if at their home
Being invited for dinner at a friend's house
Friend/relative moving into new home

Now more and more people in China also give gifts on the Western holidays such as Valentine's Day, Mother's Day, New Year's Day, and sometimes Christmas.

Traditional Chinese Festivals

There are several traditional Chinese festivals:

LANTERN FESTIVAL(Yuánxiāojié), on the fifteenth day of the Lunar New Year (in January or February), marks the end of the Spring Festival. People hang lanterns and eat boiled stuffed dumplings made of glutinous rice flour (tangyuán).

QINGMING FESTIVAL(Qīngmíngjié), on April 5, is for mourning one's ancestors. Traditional activities include sweeping off the graves of ancestors, offering sacrificial foods, and burning pieces of paper that resemble paper money for the dead to spend in their world.

DRAGON BOAT FESTIVAL(Duānwǔjié), on the fifth day of the fifth month in the lunar calendar (in April or May), commemorates the death of Qū Yuán (475BC—221 BC), the father of Chinese poetry. People eat sticky-rice dumplings steamed in lotus leaves (zòngzi). Some areas also have dragon boat races.

MID-AUTUMN FESTIVAL (Zhōngqiujié), on the fifteenth day of the eighth month in the lunar calendar (in September or October), commemorates an unsuccessful rebellion against the Mongolian rulers of the Yuan Dynasty (1271—1368). It is a festival for family reunions. On the eve of Mid-Autumn Festival, after eating dinner, people watch the moon while eating "moon cakes" (yuèbǐng) and fruits.

Communications

Public Phones

Despite the increasing prevalence of mobile phones, there are public phones on the street, at train stations, and in shops. Some hotels have public phones that use an "IC" card. Look for the sign "gongyòng diànhuà" (public phone). Most public phones in shops have an attendant to whom you pay after you make a call. There are additional service fees for long distance calls inside China and for international calls.

Telephone Cards

"IP" phone cards (and some local phone cards with different names, such as "200 Card") can be used to make calls at home and in hotel rooms. They can be used for both local and long-distance calls. They are much cheaper for international calls than any other method. You can buy them in stores, at post offices, and in hotel business centers. Before you use the card you must scratch off the covering from the code number.

"IC" phone cards are accepted only by special public phones called "cíkǎ diànhuà" (magnetic phones). The cost is the same as other public phones, with a service fee for long distance calls. You can buy an IC card at post offices, department stores, and large hotels. You cannot use an IC card to make calls at home or in a hotel room.

Discount Time Period for Long-distance Calls

In China long-distance phone calls made between 11:00 p.m. and 7:00 a.m. are half the price of calls made during business hours.

IDD Calls

IDD is an acronym for "International Direct Dial." All hotels in China at which foreigners can stay have this service. The surcharge for IDD / long distance calls is usually 15 percent at four- and five-star hotels and 10 per cent at less expensive hotels. If you want to make long distance calls from your hotel room, you must first pay a deposit at the front desk and ask the attendant to activate the long distance line in your room.

Cell Phones

Three major Chinese cell phone companies

Chinese government reorganized the Telecommunications industry in 2009 and gradually merged them into three large telecommunication companies: China Mobile (China Mobile Communications Corporation, 中国移动通信集团公司); China Unicom 中国联通 short of 中国联合网络通信集团有限公司); China TeleCom (CTC, 中国电信).

China Mobile uses TD-SCDMA, China Unicom uses CDMA2000 and China TeleCom uses WCDMA. Three have hard competition in developing 3G and trying starting 4G now.

China Mobile takes 71.5 %, China Unicom takes 20.2 % and China TeleCom takes 8.3 of the telecommunication market in China.

SIM card and cell phone recharge card

When you buy a cell phone in China, you only get a cell phone and not a telephone number with it. After you buy a cell phone, you will need to buy a SIM card from one of the three Chinese telecommunication companies: China Mobile, China Unicom or China TeleCom and insert it in your phone. With the SIM card installed you will have a phone number and can make calls. The SIM card company will charge the calls by the minute. When you have used up the money on the SIM card, you can find any news stand on the street and buy a "cell phone recharge card" (手机充值卡) to add money into your SIM card. The "cell phone recharge card" comes in denominations of 10 yuan, 20 yuan, 30 yuan, 50 yuan and 100 yuan . The card seller will be willing to help you with the recharge process. You can freely switch your phone from one company to another.

Cell phone package/combo

The term "tàocān 套餐" meaning "combo" is borrowed from the McDonalds combo meals. A cell phone package/combo provides long-term users with maximum benefits. There are many kinds of packages offered by the three telecommunication companies in China. Examples are student packages , music packages, Internet chat packages, or text message packages, for example one costing 20 yuan / month for 300 text messages and 360 minutes of calls.

Terms for types of cell phones

APPLE	Píngguǒ 苹果
Blackberry	Hēiméi 黑莓
LG	Hánguó lè jīn 韩国乐金
Motorola	Mótuōluólā 摩托罗拉
NOKIA	Nuòjīyà 诺基亚
SAMSUNG	Sānxīng 三星
SONY	Suǒní 索尼
Bar phone	zhí bǎn jī 直板机
Clamshell phone /Flip phone	fāngài jī 翻盖机
Slide phone	huá gài jī 滑盖机
Swivel phone	xuán gài shǒujī 旋盖手机

Internet Cafés

Internet cafés are very prevalent and popular in China. Sometimes, especially during school vacations, they will be filled with students playing computer games. There are two kinds of Internet cafés: officially approved Internet cafés and black market Internet cafés. The officially approved Internet cafés will ask for identification before allowing you to use the Internet. Black market Internet cafés sometimes are hidden in residential buildings and do not comply with fire safety regulations. They are not safe to use.

Membership at an Internet Café

Internet cafés usually offer two sets of fees, one for occasional use without a membership and one with lower prices if you purchase a membership. Non-members will pay about double the price of the members. For example, if you buy a 30 yuan or more Internet card, you automatically become a member of that Internet café. That 30 yuan membership card typically includes a 10 yuan membership card fee and 20 yuan for online time. Each Internet café has different fee structure.

Internet sites

Chinese Internet connections often are slower than in Western countries, but Internet usage is growing very rapidly in China, and the speed and service are improving, but service sometimes is unpredictably interrupted for several hours or longer. The Chinese government exerts strong control of Web sites and blocks access to many Web sites that are common in the West, including many government (.gov) and organization (.org) sites. The blocking of those Internet sites is variable and is not publicly announced. Many office and school networks (such as in school computer labs) prohibit the use of instant message systems.

AT THE HOSPITAL / CLINIC

Medical Registration (guàhào)

When you want to see a doctor in a hospital / clinic, the first step is to go to a window marked "挂号" (guàhào—to register). It costs about five yuán for a foreign patient. You will get a registration number and a medical record book.

Medical Examining Room

Unlike hospitals or clinics in the West, the patient will not see a nurse first. In China the doctor sits in the examining room with the door open and the patients come and go. Often there will be two doctors sharing the examining room, with each seeing a patient. The doctor will make an examination and give you a prescription. In China it is not a standard procedure to check your temperature or blood pressure before you see the doctor.

Chapter 19 Living and Teaching in China: Tips for Teachers

Payment

You will pay all the fees, including the examination fee and prescription fee, at the payment window before picking up your medicine at the pharmacy window.

Pharmacy

In China the pharmacy is in the hospital. You take your prescription and your payment receipt to the pharmacy window and give them to a pharmacist to fill the prescription while you wait at the window. The pharmacist will tell you how to take the medicine and will also give you written instructions.

Centigrade and Fahrenheit Conversion

Centigrade	Fahrenheit
38℃	100 ℉
32℃	90 ℉
11℃	52 ℉
0℃	32 ℉
-18℃	0 ℉
-29℃	-20 ℉

MANDARIN: THE STANDARD CHINESE SPEECH

You might wonder why many television programs in China are captioned with Chinese characters. The written characters are the same throughout China and wherever Chinese is spoken worldwide. But China has many regional dialects, and their pronunciation can differ as much as Italian does from Portuguese. For many centuries, in Imperial China, Mandarin was the official dialect (guānhuà), and was spoken by officials throughout China. Then in 1919 the government designated Mandarin as the "National Language" (guóyǔ), using the Beijing dialect as the standard for pronunciation and the vernacular Northern dialect as the standard for vocabulary and grammar. Since the establishment of the People's Republic of China in 1949, Mandarin has been referred to as "Common Speech" (pǔtōnghuà); Taiwan has continued to use the name "guóyǔ." Today, Mandarin is the standard Chinese speech and the official medium of communication throughout China, and is also the local spoken language in fourteen provinces and for 73 percent of the population of China.

AIR TRAVEL IN CHINA

Major airlines in China

代码 Code	航空公司 Airline	代码 Code	航空公司 Airline
CA	中国国际航空公司 Zhōngguó guójì hángkōng gōngsī Air China	WH	中国西北航空公司 Zhōngguó xīběi hángkōng gōngsī China Northwest Airlines
MU	中国东方航空股份有限公司 Zhōngguó dōngfāng hángkōng gōngsī China Eastern Airlines	CJ	中国北方航空公司 Zhōngguó běifāng hángkōng yǒuxiàn China gōngsī Northern Airlines
CZ	中国南方航空股份有限公司 Zhōngguó nánfāng hángkōng gǔfèn yǒuxiàn gōngsī China Southern Airlines	F6	中国航空股份有限公司 Zhōngguó hángkōng gǔfèn yǒuxiàn China gōngsī National Aviation
SZ	中国西南航空公司 Zhōngguó xīnán hángkōng gōngsī China Southwest Airlines	XO	新疆航空公司 Xīnjiāng hángkōng gōngsī Xinjiang Airlines
3Q	云南航空公司 Yúnnán hángkōng gōngsī Yunnan Airlines	ZH	深圳航空公司 Shēnzhèn hángkōng gōngsī Shenzhen Airlines
G4	贵州省航空公司 Guìzhōu hángkōng gōngsī Guizhou Airlines	CXI	山西航空公司 Shānxsī hángkōng gōngsī Shanxi Airlines
MF	厦门航空公司 Xiàmén hángkōng gōngsī Xiamen Airlines	H4	海南航空股份有限公司 Hǎinán hángkōng gǔ fèn yǒuxiàn gōngsī Hainan Airlines
FM	上海航空公司 Shànghǎi hángkōng gōngsī Shanghai Airlines	SC	山东航空公司 Shāndōng hángkōng gōngsī Shandong Airlines
3U	四川航空公司 Sìchuān hángkōng gōngsī Sichuan Airlines	2Z	长安航空公司 Cháng'ān hángkōng gōngsī Chang an Airlines
WU	武汉航空公司 Wǔhàn hángkōng gōngsī Wuhan Airlines	KA	港龙航空公司 Gǎngong hángkōng gōngsī Dragonair
ZJ	浙江航空公司 Zhèjiāng hángkōng gōngsī Zhejiang Airlines	X2	中国新华航空公司 Zhōngguó xīnhuá hángkōng gōngsī Chinaxinhua Airlines

Chapter 19 Living and Teaching in China: Tips for Teachers

Airline ticketing

a. Period of ticket validity

An airplane ticket in China usually has a one-year period of validity starting from the date of purchase. In other words, you can use it anytime within a year.

b. Ticket refund

If not used for any reason, a ticket can be refunded. The refund can only be done 24 hours to 2 hours before flight time. The ticket can be refunded where it was issued or at the airport. For a ticket refund, you need to have a valid ticket and identification (passport). You will be charged 10% of the ticket price. If the airline cancels, delays or changes the route, you can get a full refund. If you have note from a doctor, you can also get a full refund.

c. Lostticket

Lost tickets can be replaced if you can provide sufficient proof of purchase at least one hour before the flight. The replaced ticket cannot be refunded.

Seating

When you buy an airline ticket in China you get a "reserved seat" (定座 dìng zuò), which means you are guaranteed to have a seat and luggage space on the flight, but it does not mean you have an "assigned seat." In most cases, passengers will get their seat assignment at check-in. Some Chinese airlines have started to give seat assignments when you buy the ticket, or if you request it on the phone.

Luggage

A passenger can check 20 kilos in economy class, 30 kilos in business class, and 40 kilos in first class without restriction on number of bags. The size cannot be over 40/60/100cm. Carry-on luggage is limited to 5 kilos and 20/40/55 cm.

Overweight luggage will be charged 1.5% of the ticket price per extra kilo. The passenger gets a payment notice for his/her overweight luggage at the check-in counter, goes to another counter to pay for it, and then brings the receipt back to the check-in counter.

If the attendant at the check-in counter does not approve of a piece of luggage, you will be asked to take your luggage to a packing service counter (usually near the front door of the airport) to re-pack it and secure it with strapping tape. There is a small charge for this service.

Peak travel seasons

The peak travel seasons in China are around the Chinese national holidays:

New Year's Day: January 1-3
Spring Festival: usually in February, 7 days
Qingming Festival: April 5, 3 days
Labor Day: May 1, 3 days
Dragon Boat Festival: in May or June, 3 days
Mid-Autumn Festival: in September or October, 3 days
National Day: October 1, 7 days

Summer vacation for schools, in July and August, and the winter vacation, for about a month in January-February around the Spring Festival, are also peak travel periods.

Acronyms

ALM = Audio-Lingual Method
CLT = Communicative Language Teaching
EAP = English for Academic Purposes
EFL = English as a Foreign Language
ELL = English Language Learner
ESL = English as Second language
ESP = English for Specific Purposes
GTM = Grammar Translation Method
IEP = Intensive English Program
L1 = First Language
L2 = Second Language
Ss = Students
T = Teacher
TEFL = Teaching English as a Foreign Language
TPR = Total Physical Response

References

Anderson, R.C. and Pearson, P.D. (1984). "A schema-theoretic view of basic processes in reading comprehension," in Carrell, P. L., Devine, J. and Eskey, D. E. (eds.) (1988). *Interactive Approaches to Second Language Reading*. Cambridge: CUP.

Austin, John L. (1962). *How to Do Things with Words*.Oxford: OUP.

Brown, H. Douglas. (2006). *Principles of Language Teaching, 5th edition*. New York: Pearson ESL.

Elbow, Peter. (1975). *Writing without Teachers*. Oxford: OUP.

Ferris, Dana. (2002). *Treatment of Error in Second Language Writing*. Ann Arbor: University of Michigan Press.

McWhorter, K.T. (2007). *Reading Across Disciplines, 3rd edition*.New York: Pearson Longman.

Nunan. D. (1991). *Language Teaching Methodology*. UK: Prentice Hall International.

Pinker, Steven. (2003). *The Blank Slate: A Modern Denial of Human Nature*. New York: Penguin.

Pinker, Steven. (2007). *The Language Instinct*. New York: Harper Collins.

Searle, John R. (1975). "A Taxonomy of Illocutionary Acts", in Günderson, K. (ed.), *Language, Mind, and Knowledge*, Minneapolis, vol. 7.

Shulevitz, Uri. (1967). *One Monday Morning*. Chicago: Scribner and Sons.